Second Edition

ASSESSMENT ESSENTIALS
for
STANDARDS-BASED
EDUCATION

Second Edition

ASSESSMENT
ESSENTIALS
for
STANDARDS-BASED
EDUCATION

James H. McMillan

CORWIN PRESS
A SAGE Company
Thousand Oaks, CA 91320

For information:

Corwin Press
A SAGE Company
2455 Teller Road
Thousand Oaks, California 91320
www.corwinpress.com

SAGE Ltd.
1 Oliver's Yard
55 City Road
London EC1Y 1SP
United Kingdom

SAGE India Pvt. Ltd.
B 1/I 1 Mohan Cooperative
    Industrial Area
Mathura Road, New Delhi 110 044
India

SAGE Asia-Pacific Pte. Ltd.
33 Pekin Street #02–01
Far East Square
Singapore 048763

Printed in the United States of America.

Library of Congress Cataloging-in-Publication Data

McMillan, James H.
Assessment essentials for standards-based education/James H. McMillan.—2nd ed.
    p. cm.
Revised ed. of: Essential assessment concepts for teachers and administrators.
Includes bibliographical references and index.
ISBN 978-1-4129-5550-8 (cloth : acid-free paper)
ISBN 978-1-4129-5551-5 (pbk. : acid-free paper)
  1. Educational tests and measurements. 2. Grading and marking (Students)
3. Examinations—Validity. 4. Academic achievement—Testing. I. McMillan,
James H. Essential assessment concepts for teachers and administrators. II. Title.

LB3051.M4624987 2008
371.26—dc22   2008004899

This book is printed on acid-free paper.

08   09   10   11   12   10 9 8 7 6 5 4 3 2 1

Acquisitions Editor:	Dan Alpert
Editorial Assistant:	Tatiana Richards
Production Editor:	Eric Garner
Copy Editor:	Gretchen Treadwell
Typesetter:	C&M Digitals (P) Ltd.
Proofreader:	Theresa Kay
Indexer:	Molly Hall
Cover Designer:	Lisa Miller

Contents

Preface

This is a book that I have wanted to write for a long time. After more than 30 years in the education profession, I am convinced that a solid foundation in assessment concepts and principles is essential to effective teaching. I've seen how sound assessment can motivate students and enhance learning. I have also seen how assessment can be misused and harmful. Clearly, assessment is at the forefront of standards-based reform in education. Now, more than ever, those conducting assessments and using results need to be well-informed about what we have learned through many decades and about what standards guide our profession.

My intent in this book is to present essential assessment concepts in a concise manner that can be understood and applied by teachers, administrators, and other school personnel as they implement standards-based education and instruction. Policy makers, as well, will find the content helpful in making assessment-related decisions. To accomplish this, I have organized the chapters around major assessment topics. The first chapter provides an introduction to assessment terminology and the connections between assessment, instruction, and learning. The next three chapters introduce validity, reliability, and fairness—topics that are integral to developing high-quality assessments and to using them appropriately. Chapter 5 is new to this edition. It provides a succinct overview of different assessment techniques and methods, including both constructed-response and closed-end types of items. Chapter 6 reviews essential numerical concepts, and Chapter 7 discusses important principles of standardized testing, including standards-based standardized testing. The final chapter is also new to this edition. It concerns grading practices in the context of standards-based education.

My hope is that your reading of this book will enhance your teaching, that you will apply what is presented in your own educational context, and that students will learn more as a result. Please feel free to email me with questions, suggestions, and ideas (jmcmillan@vcu.edu).

Acknowledgments

C orwin Press would like to acknowledge the contributions of the following reviewers:

Judy Arter
Corwin Press Author
Beavercreek, OR

Diane Barone
Professor of Literacy Studies
University of Nevada
Reno, NV

Jacie Bejster
Principal
Crafton Elementary
Pittsburgh, PA

Ken O'Connor
Assess for Success Consulting
Scarborough, Ontario, Canada

Neal Glasgow
Corwin Press Author
San Dieguito School District
Encinitas, CA

About the Author

James H. McMillan is Professor and Chair of Foundations of Education at Virginia Commonwealth University in Richmond, Virginia, where he teaches educational research and assessment courses and directs the Research and Evaluation Track of the PhD in Education program. He is also Director of the Metropolitan Educational Research Consortium, a partnership of Virginia Commonwealth University and seven Richmond-area school divisions that conducts and disseminates action and applied research. His current research interests include classroom and large-scale assessment. He has recently published the fourth edition of *Classroom Assessment: Principles and Practice for Effective Standards-Based Instruction* and edited *Formative Classroom Assessment: Theory Into Practice*. He has authored three educational research methods textbooks and published numerous articles in journals, including the *American Educational Research Journal*, the *Journal of Educational Psychology*, *Contemporary Educational Psychology*, and *Educational Measurement: Issues and Practice*.

1

Integrating Assessment With Teaching and Learning

It wasn't too long ago that I was a student taking a "tests and measurement" course in my graduate program. We spent most of our time in this class learning how to construct objective classroom tests (multiple-choice, matching, and true/false) and how to interpret standardized test scores. But I really didn't see much relevance to teaching or to student learning. The emphasis was on testing after instruction to determine grades, and on using standardized test scores to see how students compared with others nationwide. I learned that measurement was separate from instruction, something that was done to document or audit student achievement. Today, however, new theories of learning, motivation, and instruction have led to a reconceptualization of measurement concepts, ideas, and principles for teachers. There is now realization that assessment, more broadly conceived, is an essential part of instruction and should be viewed as a tool not only to document learning but also to enhance learning. Whether the assessment is focused on what occurs in the classroom or on externally mandated standardized tests, teachers need to know how to effectively integrate assessment with teaching and learning so that it enhances learning and the attainment of overall educational goals.

Recently, I had an opportunity to interview some teachers about their classroom assessments and grading. Here is what a few of them said:

- To me, grades are extremely secondary to the whole process of what we do. I have goals to what I want to teach, and I use assessment so that I know what I need to work on, what people have mastered, and what they haven't.
- I've changed to using more group assessments. If you really want a student to learn, the student has to be actively engaged and doing group work. I find that works best. You can just see the lights go on with the kids.
- When they come in, you give them a pop quiz. It reinforces what they learned the day before.
- It'll go back to the goal I have: Try to meet the needs, interests, and capabilities of the children. If you don't have a variety of assessments, you're not really focusing on what the students' abilities are.
- I always assess early on to see what people know so that I can split groups as needed. I am a real stickler for assessing only to find out what people know and what they've learned.
- Assessments where they actually have to show me some work or write about what they know are most valuable . . . Because it's then that you know that they understood every process. That tells you a lot more about a student than just grading a sheet of answers.

As you can see, these teachers, who represent a range of experience and subject matter, think about classroom assessments and grading as components of instruction. They don't separate "testing" and grading from instruction. Rather, they see instruction and assessment as integrated aspects of teaching, each depending on the other. This is an important departure point for deciding what constitutes "essential measurement concepts." My view is that what is most basic to assessment is what is fundamental to understanding and enhancing student learning. After all, isn't this what education is all about?

Although there are different definitions of assessment in the literature, the one by Peter Airasian (1997) is especially good: "Assessment is the process of collecting, synthesizing, and interpreting information to aid in decision making" (p. 3). I like this definition because it conveys clearly and succinctly different aspects that make up the complete process of "assessment." This is a contemporary view. In the past, assessment tended to be equated more or less with testing and the simple gathering of information. The broader, more inclusive, definition is better because it places such tasks as making up a test, administering it, and scoring the results in a larger context that includes interpretation and use of the results.

Although classroom assessment focuses on what teachers do daily to influence student learning, standardized testing can also be used to enhance student performance. Ironically, at the same time that increased emphasis has been placed on classroom assessments, standardized tests are being used with greater frequency to verify student performance and accredit schools. Consequently, teachers and administrators need a thorough understanding of fundamental concepts and principles of both classroom assessment and standardized testing to effectively apply these tools to improve student achievement.

In this chapter, I will take you through what I consider to be essential concepts that link assessment, instruction, and learning. I'll need to define some terms to lay the groundwork for later applications but will spend most of the chapter showing how assessment, in its many forms, and instruction and learning are inexorably intertwined. First, let's consider implications of standards-based education.

THE ROLE OF ASSESSMENT IN STANDARDS-BASED EDUCATION

For the past two decades, American education has been dominated by "standards." This emphasis is often referred to as "standards-based." The emphasis on standards resulted from dissatisfaction with the state of education, with what students know and can do. The consensus among many politicians was that students were not obtaining the level of knowledge and understanding needed to be competitive with other countries. The standards movement has also focused on the need to educate all students to reduce achievement gaps. Thus, there is a recognition that we need *higher* standards for *all* students. This has led to the development of both *content* standards and *performance* standards. Content standards define the essential knowledge, understandings, and skills. They have been developed for all states. Performance standards (benchmarks) represent the levels of performance defined in the content standards that establish specific expectations and examples of what it means to be "proficient" or "adequate" in what is demonstrated by the students. This, in turn, has led to testing student learning according to content and performance standards. And thus, testing has led to accountability.

New ideas about accountability for teachers, schools, school districts, and states have been adopted to promote the inculcation of standards-based education. The No Child Left Behind legislation has put teeth into accountability by requiring schools to demonstrate adequate progress on student achievement. We now have a system that requires high student achievement on tests, tied to such sanctions as grade retention, high school graduation, and school accreditation, which has coined the term "high-stakes testing."

Standards-based education, with increased testing requirements and accountability, has made a profound and ubiquitous impact in the classroom. Content is more standardized, with curriculum pacing guides used by all teachers in the same grade and content areas. Classroom tests are aligned with the content standards and accountability tests, often resulting in the use of classroom test questions that are like the items in accountability tests—multiple-choice. Teachers are under significant pressure to ensure high test scores.

From my perspective, any discussion of educational assessment must include a consideration of what the standards-based and accountability movement has meant for schools, classrooms, and teachers. The movement has had such a dramatic impact that it makes sense to consider assessment in two major ways—as large-scale, and as local. *Large-scale* tests are those that are prepared for assessing hundreds and thousands of students. Historically, such tests were identified as standardized achievement tests and ability tests. Today, though, large-scale tests are more likely to be those used by a state or school district to measure student learning for accountability. These tests are developed by professionals for use across many classrooms, and, with the exception of the testing of writing, are mostly multiple choice. They are "external" to the classroom.

In contrast, *local* assessments are tests, observations, ratings, and other forms of evidence used by teachers *in their classroom*, or by teachers *in their school*. Of course, teachers have always tested students! What is important is that recent cognitive and constructivist theories of student learning and motivation suggest that certain assessment strategies in the classroom will be effective (see Figure 1.1 for recent trends). The trouble is that many of these are in direct contradiction to the influence of standards-based accountability testing. Teachers and principals are literally caught in the middle of these conflicting influences. Clearly, teachers, principals, and other school personnel need to understand and effectively use fair and accurate ways in both local and large-scale assessments. Each is essential in education today. Fortunately, we have considerable research about, and experience with, each kind of assessment so that student learning is enhanced as well as documented.

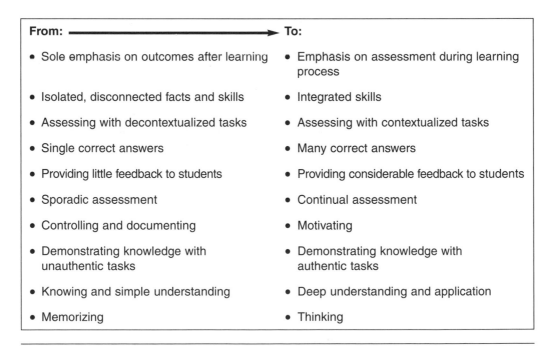

From: ———————————————▶	To:
• Sole emphasis on outcomes after learning	• Emphasis on assessment during learning process
• Isolated, disconnected facts and skills	• Integrated skills
• Assessing with decontextualized tasks	• Assessing with contextualized tasks
• Single correct answers	• Many correct answers
• Providing little feedback to students	• Providing considerable feedback to students
• Sporadic assessment	• Continual assessment
• Controlling and documenting	• Motivating
• Demonstrating knowledge with unauthentic tasks	• Demonstrating knowledge with authentic tasks
• Knowing and simple understanding	• Deep understanding and application
• Memorizing	• Thinking

Figure 1.1   Recent Trends in the Purpose of Classroom Assessments

Source: Adapted from *Classroom Assessment: Principles and Practice for Effective Standards-Based Instruction* (2nd ed.), by J. H. McMillan, 2007, Boston: Allyn & Bacon. Copyright © by Allyn & Bacon. Adapted with permission.

Assessment and Effective Teaching

With some reflection, it is not hard to see how assessment is essential to teaching. Teaching is a process of effective decision making. This includes deciding what to teach, how to teach it, how long to teach, whether to group students, what questions to ask, what follow-up questions to ask, what to review, when to review, and so forth. Figure 1.2 illustrates the nature of decisions according to when the decisions are made—before, during, or after instruction. This is a useful way to think about teacher decision making because it organizes the decisions by the sequence teachers use.

Each decision that is made needs to be based on something. Typically, teachers use their experience, logical reasoning, and tradition, among other sources of knowledge, to make their decisions. Assessment of students is critical because effective decision making is based to some extent on the ability of teachers to understand their students and to match actions with accurate assessments. Can you imagine a doctor deciding on a prescription without a complete understanding of the patient? Likewise, teachers need to understand students before they can choose instructional methods and give students grades. In other words, effective teachers include both local and large-scale assessment as sources of information that empowers evidence-based interpretations, decisions, and actions (Moss, Girard, & Haniford, 2006).

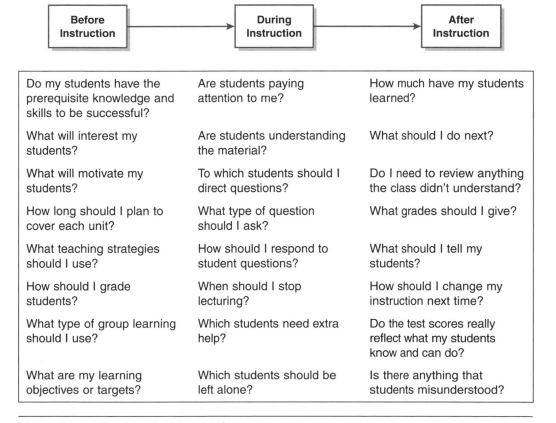

Before Instruction	During Instruction	After Instruction
Do my students have the prerequisite knowledge and skills to be successful?	Are students paying attention to me?	How much have my students learned?
What will interest my students?	Are students understanding the material?	What should I do next?
What will motivate my students?	To which students should I direct questions?	Do I need to review anything the class didn't understand?
How long should I plan to cover each unit?	What type of question should I ask?	What grades should I give?
What teaching strategies should I use?	How should I respond to student questions?	What should I tell my students?
How should I grade students?	When should I stop lecturing?	How should I change my instruction next time?
What type of group learning should I use?	Which students need extra help?	Do the test scores really reflect what my students know and can do?
What are my learning objectives or targets?	Which students should be left alone?	Is there anything that students misunderstood?

Figure 1.2   Teacher Decision Making

Purposes of Assessment

There are many reasons to assess students. Teachers want to know how much students understand before they begin a unit of instruction, how much students are progressing in their understanding during instruction, and how much students have learned at the end of a unit. Special education teachers need assessments to prescribe specific instructional strategies. Principals want to know how students in their school score on standardized tests. Parents want assessment information to see how well their children are doing in school. Policy makers need assessment data to make judgments about the quality of education that students receive. Colleges need student scores on admissions tests to make admissions decisions.

Assessment begins, then, with identification of the specific purpose for collecting and interpreting the information. Once the purpose has been identified, appropriate methods for gathering and synthesizing the information can be identified. What works well for one purpose may not work well for another. This is an important lesson about assessment: *The nature of the assessment method should follow from the intended purpose.*

Local and Large-Scale Assessments

In thinking about purpose, it is helpful to differentiate local (classroom) assessment from large-scale assessment (school district, state, and national). Both may have the same ultimate goal, to improve student learning, but the more immediate purposes, methods, and use of results differ in significant ways. The purposes of local assessment are focused on teacher decision making and include the following (not a complete list):

- To identify if students have mastered a concept or skill
- To motivate students to be more engaged in learning
- To get students to learn the content in a way that stresses application and other reasoning skills
- To help develop a positive attitude about a subject
- To communicate to parents what students know and can do
- To communicate expectations to students
- To give students feedback about what they know and can do
- To show students what they need to focus on to improve their understanding
- To encourage student self-evaluation
- To determine report card grades
- To evaluate the effectiveness of instructional approaches

Large-scale assessments have different immediate purposes (not all of which are desirable):

- To evaluate the effectiveness of a new curriculum
- To identify student strengths and weaknesses
- To compare different schools or school divisions

- To evaluate teachers
- To provide information for school accreditation
- To see how students as a group do in comparison with a national sample of students
- To evaluate principals
- To determine if students are meeting state or national "standards"
- To determine how to group students
- To allocate resources
- To identify students with special needs

Once the purpose is identified, a critical question needs to be asked, namely, *What evidence is needed to provide the best information to meet the stated purpose?* This seemingly simple question lies at the heart of high-quality decision making. There are many choices in the nature of the evidence. Let's look at an example with classroom assessment. Suppose you are a teacher and have identified the following purpose: "to give students feedback to enable them to improve their skill in multiplying fractions." Now, what type of assessment will best meet this purpose? Should the assessment be done in class or at home? Should a quiz use multiple-choice questions or constructed-response questions (for which students show their work)? Should students get credit for knowing the process but not getting the correct answer because of faulty arithmetic?

To answer these questions, we need to focus on the students' learning process. Assessments done in class (where parents can't help) that require students to show their work would provide stronger evidence of what students can do than would homework or multiple-choice tests. The former would give the teacher an opportunity to diagnose misunderstandings to pinpoint immediate feedback that is individualized and specific to the task. Thus, the constructed-response items meet the stated purpose much better than would homework or a multiple-choice test.

An important distinction to keep in mind between the purposes of local classroom assessment and large-scale assessment is that local classroom assessment is focused on the individual student and how to provide the best information to maximize student learning in a particular classroom. Large-scale assessment, on the other hand, emphasizes group data, typically at the school, district, or state level. These and other differences are summarized in Table 1.1.

Formative and Summative Assessment

One very helpful way to categorize different purposes of assessment is to use the terms *formative* and *summative*. The purpose of formative assessment is to improve student learning; it is assessment *for* student learning. In contrast, summative assessment is used to document student learning; it is assessment *of* learning. Formative assessment is designed to extend and encourage learning; summative assessment is used to determine how much students have learned, with little or no emphasis on using the results to improve learning. See Table 1.2 for a summary of characteristics of summative and formative assessment.

Table 1.1   Differences Between Local Classroom and Large-Scale Assessment

Local Classroom Assessment	Standardized, Large-Scale Assessment
Focused on individual students	Focused on groups of students
Conducted before, during, and after instruction	Conducted before and after instruction
Teacher-made	Made by outside "experts"
Tailored to individual classes	Same items for all students
Immediate individualized feedback to students	Delayed general feedback to students
May be timed or untimed	Usually timed
Given continuously	Given sporadically
Tends to cover short units	Tends to cover a large domain of content
Compares scores with levels of performance	Tends to report scores compared with other students
Weak technical properties such as reliability	Strong technical properties
Used for grading students and improvement	Used for teacher and school accountability

Table 1.2   Characteristics of Formative and Summative Assessment

Characteristic	Formative	Summative
Purpose	To provide ongoing feedback and adjustments to instruction	To document student learning at the end of an instructional segment
When Conducted	During instruction and after instruction	After instruction
Student Involvement	Encouraged	Discouraged
Student Motivation	Intrinsic, mastery-oriented	Extrinsic, performance-oriented
Teacher Role	To provide immediate, specific feedback and instructional correctives	To measure student achievement and give grades
Learning Emphasized	Deep understanding, application, and reasoning	Knowledge and comprehension
Level of Specificity	Highly specific and individual	General and group oriented
Structure	Flexible, adaptable	Rigid, highly structured
Techniques	Informal	Formal
Impact on Learning	Strong, positive, long-lasting	Weak and fleeting

Source: Adapted from McMillan (2007b).

Formative assessment can be defined more specifically as, "All those activities undertaken by teachers, and by their students in assessing themselves, which provide information to be used a feedback to modify the teaching and learning activities in which they are engaged. Such assessment becomes 'formative assessment' when the evidence is actually used to adapt the teaching work to meet the needs" (Black & Wiliam, 1998, p. 2). That is, formative assessment has a specific goal (improve learning and motivation), achieved by gathering and using information so that new instruction and experiences will lead to enhanced achievement. Carefully gathered and interpreted evidence of student performance is used continuously to inform the teacher about student progress as learning occurs, and to identify next steps (McMillan, 2007b). There is a cycle of teacher and student evaluations, feedback to students, and instructional correctives, as illustrated in Figure 1.3.

Formative assessment occurs at three points of instruction: (1) during instruction; (2) between lessons; and (3) between units. Most formative assessment occurs during instruction (Wiliam & Leahy, 2007). This is when teachers are actively engaged in assessing student progress as they instruct. Here teachers are observing and using questions, giving feedback in informal, targeted ways. Between lessons teachers use formative assessment to inform what

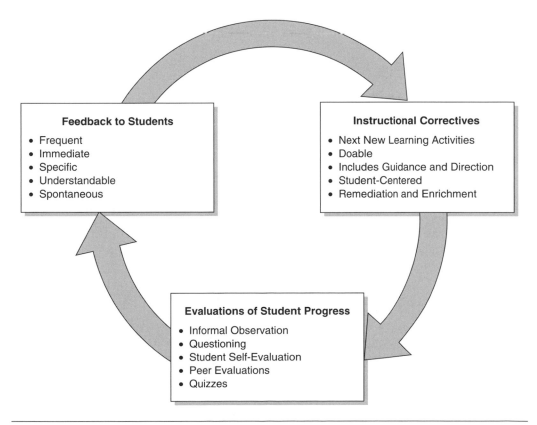

Figure 1.3   Formative Assessment Cycle

Source: Adapted from McMillan (2007b).

subsequent lessons will accomplish. This is typically based on quizzes, observation, student self-assessment, and other data that represent important short-term milestones. Units represent blocks of learning that occur weekly or monthly. While more cumulative tests and other major assessment are given at the end of these time frames, they are designed to give feedback to the teacher to help determine the nature of the next unit.

Summative assessments are done at the end of a period of learning (lessons, units, years) for the purpose of documenting student proficiency at the time of the assessment. Student achievement is monitored and recorded, as is the case with large-scale accountability testing and standardized testing.

As illustrated in Figure 1.4, teachers use both formative and summative assessment, and many test publishers believe they can provide both types of information. Actually, formative assessment has become such a buzzword that large testing companies now advertise that they can provide teachers with "banks" of items that can be used in a formative manner. They say that they provide "formative assessment." As pointed out by Popham (2006), however, what such publishers say and what the assessments do is inconsistent with what formative assessment is all about. Typically, such "benchmark" tests are "mini-summative" in nature, without the key aspects of formative assessment that involve providing feedback (other than how many items were answered correctly) or that suggest new instructional activities. For instance, Educational Testing Service (ETS) now offers what they call a "formative assessment test bank." ETS claims that their items are aligned to state standards, have excellent technical quality, are classified by Bloom's cognitive levels, and have a full

	Formative	*Summative*
Local (Classroom)	Homework Quiz Paper Project Observation Questioning Feedbacks	Chapter test Semester exam Final paper Report Presentation
Large-Scale	Test "banks"	Graduation test State standards-based test National Assessment of Educational Progress Standardized achievement tests Ability tests

Figure 1.4 Examples of Formative and Summative Assessments in Local and Large-Scale Contexts

range of difficulty. Such claims, however, do not mean that use of test banks will be helpful. Buyer beware is an apt perspective, and pilot testing is recommended before a commitment to full implementation.

Nebraska is a good example of how large-scale accountability testing can take on a local flavor. School districts in that state were required to construct their own student assessments that would measure student progress toward established standards. School-based Teacher-led Assessment and Reporting System, called STARS, allows local districts and schools both the responsibility and flexibility of designing and implementing the accountability tests. While this may "localize" the assessments, if they are still primarily summative in nature, feedback and use of instructional correctives may not be provided. This type of program surely promotes two outcomes: teachers learn a lot about testing and how to use test data, and having accountability tests generate from teachers up, rather than from companies down, may be economical!

Method of Measurement or Description

Once the purpose of assessment has been identified, a method of measuring the trait or skill of interest needs to be selected. Assessment methods can be divided into two major categories—those that use measurement and those that use nonnumerical description. The term *measurement* is used to describe the process by which traits, attributes, performance, behavior, and characteristics (I'll use the single term *trait* to refer to all of these) are *differentiated* by assigning different numbers to represent the degree to which the trait is possessed by or demonstrated by an individual. This is essentially asking *how much* of something is observed and using some scale to quantify the extent of it. Thus, teachers administer tests and score them to record the measurement of the trait, for example, a "70" or "94." Similarly, on a standardized test, a score may be reported as a raw score of the number of items answered correctly, the percentage of items answered correctly, a "standard" score, or a percentile rank. In each case, numbers are generated from some type of test or performance to represent the degree to which the trait is present. This is called *quantitative* assessment.

Traits are also differentiated through the use of verbal descriptions, rather than or in addition to numbers. This is termed *qualitative* assessment. Words, rather than numbers, are used to differentiate the traits. For example, teachers may describe performance by pointing out what was included, appropriately, and what was missing. Here are two illustrations of this type of description:

> *"John, you have used the correct formula to solve the problem but did not subtract accurately."*

> *"Kim, the project you submitted demonstrated a complete understanding of different types of trees. Your conclusions would be better if you mentioned all types of trees."*

Many newer types of assessments describe different levels or degrees of performance verbally and then assign numbers to each level, for example:

1	2	3	4
Has a severely limited range of complex thinking skills for managing complex tasks	Demonstrates ability in a number of complex thinking processes but does not have a full complement of skills for managing complex issues	Demonstrates competency in a number of complex thinking processes and usually applies the processes effectively	Demonstrates mastery of a variety of complex thinking processes and consistently applies the processes effectively

The measurement and description process includes both the procedures for collecting information and the assigning of numbers or verbal narratives to represent different degrees of the trait.

The procedures for collecting information can vary, from something structured and formal, such as an objective test, to something unstructured and informal, such as teacher observation. Table 1.3 summarizes different types of measurement and descriptive techniques. These techniques have been classified as *traditional* or *alternative* to highlight the changing nature of educational assessment. Traditional assessments are those that were developed to measure traits with paper-and-pencil tests, such as multiple-choice tests and essay tests. Alternative assessments refer to those that provide a stronger link between instruction and assessment and make learning more relevant. This is consistent with recent constructivist research that emphasizes the importance of constructing responses in relation to existing knowledge, as well as the recognition that effective education develops students' thinking and reasoning skills in addition to mastery of content (Cizek, 1997; Tombari & Borich, 1999). *Authentic assessments* are constructed to be consistent with what people do in situations that occur naturally outside the classroom. In *performance assessments,* students are required to demonstrate a skill or proficiency by creating, producing, or doing something. This occurs when students complete a project, give a speech, paint a picture, build a model home, or write a letter to the editor of a newspaper. Demonstrations or exhibitions are also types of performance assessments. *Portfolio assessments* are collections of student work that illustrate performance and improvement through time. Peer and self-assessment are now being used to involve students more directly in interpreting their work and determining what needs to be done to improve their performance.

Types of measurements and descriptions can also be categorized as *selected-response* or *constructed-response* (sometimes called *supply type*). With selected-response items, the examinee chooses an answer from those provided, as with

Table 1.3   Classifying Methods of Assessment

	Traditional	*Alternative*
Selected-response	Multiple-choice True/false Matching Binary-choice Structured observation Structured interview Surveys	Student self-assessment Peer assessment
Constructed-response	Sentence completion Short answer Essay Anecdotal observation Unstructured interview Papers Reports	Authentic assessment Performance assessment (exhibitions, demonstrations) Portfolio assessment Student self-assessment

multiple-choice, true/false, and matching. In a constructed-response assessment, students literally construct, rather than choose, a response. Constructed-response examples include short-answer items, completing a project, and giving a speech. Sometimes, selected-response assessments are called "objective" tests, whereas constructed-response assessments may be called "subjective" tests. This difference, however, refers only to the manner in which the answers are scored. Thus, a sentence completion item is a constructed-response question, but the scoring may be primarily objective if only a single answer is correct. Other constructed-response items, such as essays, may have more than one correct response and therefore are judged subjectively.

In Table 1.3, alternative assessments are completely constructed-response, whereas traditional measurement techniques may be either selected- or constructed-response. This highlights an important trend—but not one without controversy. Some maintain that traditional assessment techniques, because they have been around a long time, are tried-and-tested methods that are both familiar and trustworthy. Others argue that these same measures cannot begin to adequately assess more important skills. The significant thing to remember is that there are advantages and disadvantages to both traditional and alternative assessments, and that it is most crucial to match the type of assessment with the purpose. Always begin with purpose, and, with a knowledge of assessment options, select and implement the one(s) that will provide the best evidence.

Evaluation

After the appropriate method of assessment has been administered, the numbers or descriptions that are gathered must be interpreted. The interpretation involves making a judgment about the quality of what is gathered. This is essentially an evaluation of what has been performed. By *evaluation*, I mean a judgment about the worth or value of the performance. There is an *interpretation* of what the results mean and how they can be used. Teachers typically make these evaluations on how student performance compares with the learning objective. This is often referred to as a *criterion-referenced* or *standards-referenced* interpretation. Performance is compared with a standard or levels of performance that have been designated.

Consider as an example the following learning objective: "Students will understand the process of photosynthesis." The teacher asks students to describe photosynthesis in two paragraphs. A criterion-referenced evaluation is made by comparing each student's response with criteria that have been identified as essential to understanding photosynthesis. If a student has clearly mastered every aspect of photosynthesis, an evaluation may be "excellent," whereas partial understanding may be termed "good." Because all students are compared with levels of understanding, the evaluation does not depend at all on how students compare with each other.

With *norm-referenced* assessments, the scores are evaluated by how students compare with each other or with some other group of students. Thus, if a student scores as well as half of the comparison group, the evaluation might be that the student has demonstrated "average" knowledge or understanding. For students who score better than most, the evaluation might be "excellent." But these interpretations do not indicate much about the actual level of knowledge or understanding. With norm-referenced assessments, evaluators need to examine the questions carefully to know the level of performance that is demonstrated, as well as the nature of the group that is used for comparison. For years, most standardized testing has reported norm-referenced scores, which are less useful for improving teaching and learning than are criterion-referenced scores.

Use

Once the information gathered has been evaluated, it is used to meet the purpose for which it was intended. That is, it is used to make decisions about students, instruction, curriculum, teachers, and schools. Classroom assessments are typically put to two uses. One is to inform the teacher about how much students know and understand so that appropriate instructional interventions can be planned and implemented to enhance learning. A second use is based on documenting what students have learned, resulting in grades and report cards to inform students, parents, and others about student progress. Standardized, large-scale assessments are put to many uses, including accrediting schools, qualifying students for graduation, and evaluating curriculum.

What is important is that the way the results are used needs to be consistent with assessment methods and evaluations. For example, the results from constructed-response formats with criterion/standards-referenced evaluations are best when using assessments to give informative and motivating feedback to students. Results from selected-response formats with norm-referenced evaluations are best when assessing achievement of a large body of knowledge in relation to a national sample of students.

TEACHERS' ASSESSMENT DECISION MAKING

As with other types of decision making, teachers are influenced by a variety of factors when they decide when and how to assess students. Research has found that teachers are influenced by two types of factors (McMillan, 1999). The first is essentially internal to each teacher, consisting of teacher beliefs and values. The second is external, pressuring teachers to adopt certain assessment practices. Teacher beliefs and values that influence assessment decision making include the following:

- Philosophy of teaching (e.g., believing that all students can learn and believing in challenging students)
- Pulling for students (wanting students to be successful)
- Motivation and engagement (believing that motivation and engagement are essential to learning)
- Promoting student understanding (wanting students to truly understand concepts, principles, and skills, rather than merely showing rote memory or recognition)
- Accommodating individual differences among students (using different instructional strategies and assessments with students differing in aptitude, knowledge, learning style, attitudes, and other characteristics)

These teacher beliefs and values focus on what is best for student learning and provide the foundation for making assessment decisions. Thus, teachers may use constructed-response test items rather than selected-response items because the constructed-response items give a better measure of student understanding. Teachers may give extra credit to enable students to "pull up" low grades. Because of individual differences in students, teachers may use different types of assessments in a single class so that everyone has a chance of being successful. Performance assessments may be used because they motivate and engage students more effectively than multiple-choice tests.

External factors also affect how teachers assess students. These factors are not controllable. They represent reality in that they must be considered, but they may have effects that teachers may view as undesirable. External factors include the following:

- Mandated statewide or large-scale high-stakes accountability standardized tests
- Parental pressure (e.g., demands for verification of student performance that led to a low grade)
- District grading policies (guidelines that restrict teachers to certain procedures)
- Practical constraints (e.g., number of students, time needed to grade papers, and diversity of students served)

Although teacher beliefs and values stress what is best for learning, these external pressures are usually more oriented to auditing student learning (summative).

Clearly, mandated statewide accountability testing has changed classroom assessment so that it is more aligned with the format of the statewide test. If a high-stakes test uses a multiple-choice format, as most do, then teachers are pressured to use multiple-choice classroom tests. Teachers want to be able to show parents "objective" evidence of student performance to defend grades, and district policies may restrict the nature and use of different assessments. Practical constraints limit what teachers can realistically do. Although extensive authentic performance assessments might be best, they might not be feasible in light of other instructional needs.

As you can see, teacher beliefs and values often conflict with external pressures, especially when the teacher—or administrator, for that matter—focuses on enhancing student learning, and external pressures are focused on auditing student learning. This constant tension shapes the assessment environment in a school and in classrooms and helps in understanding *why* specific assessment practices are used, and *how* the practices affect student learning.

How can teachers and administrators ease the tension brought about from these two factors to result in a balanced and positive assessment environment? Here are a few suggestions.

1. Be crystal clear about *all* the educational goals of the state, district, school, and classroom teacher.

2. Gather and report evidence on all educational goals (not just the more visible state goals).

3. Consistently check the alignment between assessment purpose and method.

4. Make sure that teachers and administrators understand what it takes to generate *high-quality* assessments.

5. Avoid inappropriate uses of statewide assessments (e.g., for teacher or principal evaluations).

6. Treat teachers and administrators as professionals who need autonomy, support, and trust.

7. Don't allow statewide assessments to dominate local school practices.

ASSESSMENT STANDARDS FOR TEACHERS AND ADMINISTRATORS

Teachers rely on assessment to provide information that will inform and improve instruction. Because teachers play varied roles within the school, they need to be knowledgeable and competent in assessment practices that are used in these roles. In 1990, four professional organizations (the American Association of Colleges of Teacher Education, the American Federation of Teachers, the National Council on Measurement in Education, and the National

Education Association) agreed to a set of seven assessment competencies needed by teachers (Standards, 1990). These seven areas include the following:

1. Teachers should be skilled in choosing assessment methods that are appropriate for instructional decisions, depending on technical adequacy, usefulness, convenience, and fairness.

2. Teachers should be skilled in developing all types of assessments.

3. Teachers should be skilled in administering, scoring, and interpreting both standardized tests and classroom assessments.

4. Teachers should be skilled in using assessment results to make decisions about individual students, instruction, curriculum, and school improvement.

5. Teachers should be skilled in developing rational, justifiable, and fair procedures for grading students.

6. Teachers should be skilled in communicating assessment results to students, parents, additional lay audiences, and other educators.

7. Teachers should recognize and practice sound ethics and legal requirements.

There is also a set of guidelines for school administrators, also recently developed by four professional organizations (the National Council on Measurement in Education, the American Association of School Administrators, the National Association of Elementary School Principals, and the National Association of Secondary School Principals; Impara & Plake, 1996). Administrators should have the following ten administrator assessment competencies:

1. Understand assessment standards for teachers.

2. Understand and apply basic precepts of assessment and measurement theory.

3. Understand different purposes of different types of assessments.

4. Understand and communicate measurement terminology.

5. Recognize appropriate and inappropriate uses of assessments and follow ethical guidelines.

6. Know how to construct appropriate and useful assessments.

7. Know how to accurately interpret and appropriately use assessment results.

8. Understand how interpretation of assessment results is moderated by student characteristics.

9. Be able to evaluate an assessment program or strategy.

10. Use computer-based assessment tools.

What is your current self-assessment of level of understanding and skill in these competencies? Together, the two lists cover a lot! Furthermore, becoming competent in these standards requires initial understanding, followed by application in which feedback can be provided to increase depth of understanding. Yet, knowing the competencies now gives you an initial feel for the assessment landscape. The remaining chapters will examine more specific assessment principles that relate to most of these competencies, for both teachers and administrators. The purpose is to cover the basic, fundamental assessment concepts and principles that will equip you to be a more effective assessor and educator.

2

Validity

We have seen that assessment consists of collecting, interpreting, and using information in decision making and that assessment can be used to improve instruction and enhance learning, as well as to document student performance. Thinking about assessment in this way has important implications for how a familiar concept—*validity*—is defined and applied.

WHAT IS VALIDITY?

Validity can be defined as an overall evaluation that supports the intended interpretation, use, and consequences of the obtained scores. This evaluation is at the heart of high-quality assessment. Strong validity is demonstrated when evidence and logic suggest that the evaluation is accurate and reasonable. In other words, validity concerns the soundness, trustworthiness, or legitimacy of the inferences or claims that are made on the basis of the obtained scores. Obviously, better decisions will be made when the inferences or claims are accurate. Thus, the interpretations, uses, and consequences—not the test, instrument, or procedure used to gather the information—have some degree of validity. Often, the phrase "the validity of the test" is used, but it is more accurate to say "the validity of the inference from test scores." Clearly, validity is not a characteristic of a test or instrument that accompanies the test or instrument wherever and whenever it is administered. Tests are not valid; only inferences can be valid, and it's always a matter of degree, not a dichotomous distinction.

As shown in Figure 2.1, assessments are administered within a context or setting to obtain scores; the scores are then used to make claims, meanings, interpretations, and so forth. Thus, validity is a judgment, based on available

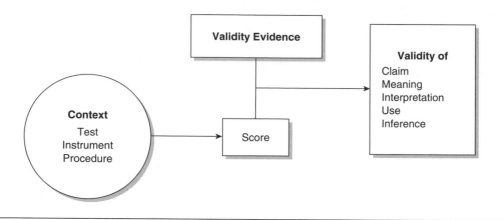

Figure 2.1   Nature of Validity

evidence, about the accuracy and reasonableness of the claim or other use within the given context (Moss, Girard, & Haniford, 2006). Let's look at a couple of examples. The same steps are used for both local classroom and large-scale assessments.

Mr. Taylor decides to assign a research project to students in his math class. Students are asked to construct a model house with five rooms, including doors and windows, that will have a given inside wall space in square feet (according to scale). Each student must construct the house in class within a week. Students are graded on whether the house is complete and accurate according to scale and with respect to total square feet. Mr. Taylor believes that this is a good assessment procedure and that students with a high grade (score) have demonstrated mastery of being able to calculate square footage (evaluation). The validity questions are these: How accurate and reasonable is the conclusion that students who score high have mastered this skill? How does Mr. Taylor know?

In Greenville County, the superintendent decides to institute a new evaluation system for teachers. She decides to use student test scores from the norm-referenced, standardized test given to students each spring as an indicator of teacher effectiveness. In other words, the test scores are used to infer whether teachers are effective. The validity questions here are these: How reasonable is it to use standardized test scores for measuring teacher effectiveness? Is it actually true (accurate) that teachers whose students score high are more effective than teachers whose students score low?

A common misconception about validity is that it is simply "the extent to which a test measures what it is supposed, or purported, to measure." Although the substance of the test is important for validity, substance is just one aspect that is involved in making a proper inference. For example, results from a test of student knowledge about algebra may be valid as an assessment of current competence but not valid for predicting achievement. A biology test may provide scores that could be valid for making decisions about content that needs to be retaught but invalid for inferring that students can reason or can read well.

Table 2.1 provides an overview of the nature of validity by summarizing important characteristics. In this table, one of the characteristics refers to validity as a "singular" concept. Some years ago, different types of validity were often referenced (e.g., content-related validity and criterion-related validity). Today, however, validity is considered to be a unitary idea, with different sources of validity evidence. For both large-scale and classroom assessments, test developers bear the responsibility of providing evidence that the stated uses of the test are valid. The test user, however, has ultimate responsibility for establishing validity for the particular setting in which test is used. If the use of test results differs from what has been identified by the test developer, then the local user has added responsibility for gathering appropriate evidence. For example, suppose that a state's student competency exam has been developed to ascertain student proficiency. If this test is used to evaluate teachers, this use needs to be supported by evidence gathered by the user. For most classroom tests, the teacher has the primary responsibility to gather evidence that the scores from the tests are appropriate indicators for specific uses, such as grades and instructional decisions (Whittington, 1999).

Table 2.1   Characteristics of Validity

- Validity is a matter of overall professional judgment.
- Validity refers to the accuracy of inferences, not to the test or procedure itself.
- Validity is specific to particular uses in particular contexts.
- Validity is not an "all or none" judgment but a matter of degree.
- Validity is a singular concept.
- Validity is established with different types of evidence.
- Validity is the joint responsibility of test developer and test user.

HOW IS VALIDITY DETERMINED?

Developing a strong case for validity involves a number of steps. It begins with a clear statement of the intended interpretations, claims, uses, or meanings for an assessment. (This statement typically includes a rationale for how that interpretation or meaning is related to the use of the scores.) Once the statement is complete, evidence is accumulated to support the legitimacy and accuracy of the intended use. In education, the proposed interpretation, meaning, or claim is closely tied to the content or skills being taught. Here are some examples of interpretations related to content or skills:

- The assessment will indicate whether the students have mastered multiplying fractions.
- The assessment will show how much students know about the Vietnam War.
- The assessment will show which components of experimentation students understand.

- The assessment will indicate how much students know about U.S. history in comparison with other students in the country.
- The assessment will indicate whether students are able to follow the appropriate steps to determine the volume of an object placed in water.

Often, interpretations involve a *construct,* an abstract conception of a trait or characteristic, such as intelligence, self-esteem, attitudes, reasoning ability, anxiety, and values. With constructs, it is important to identify the specific intended meaning. For example, attitudes may consist of feelings and/or perceptions of importance. To make a proper interpretation, the user needs to know whether a specific attitude survey measured feelings or perceptions of importance. Here are some examples of interpretations related to constructs:

- The assessment will indicate the extent to which students are motivated to learn.
- The assessment will indicate the climate of Mr. Tate's fifth-grade classroom.
- The assessment will identify the students with the lowest self-esteem.

Once the intended claim, interpretation, or inference is determined, the user gathers evidence to support the validity of the claim. The accumulated evidence is what establishes validity. When examining the types of evidence that can be used, it is helpful, I believe, to separate validity involving large-scale assessment from what teachers and administrators use for classroom and other local assessments. Much of the fairly technical language and many of the concepts and approaches to validity were developed for large-scale standardized testing, not for classroom assessment. The specific categories I will be using to present different types of evidence are based on standards for large-scale and psychological assessments. Although the same categories of evidence can be used for both large-scale and classroom assessments, teachers typically use much less formal applications in the classroom. Whether the evidence is systematic and statistical, or informal, the key to validity is that the evidence is appropriate for the type of inference that is made.

I would like to make one more point before moving on to different sources of validity evidence. An important assumption when making an inference about what a student knows, understands, and can do is that the student tried as much as possible to do well on the test. The motivation, effort, persistence, and seriousness that students bring to the testing situation all contribute to the scores. If we, as teachers or administrators, are not certain about these factors, then our inferences may well be invalid. Take the situation of a state competency exam that is used for school accreditation but has no implications for individual students. How seriously would students take the test, especially if the students are in high school? If they don't try hard, interpreting low scores to mean that the students do not know the content well would be invalid. Or, consider a measure of student attitudes. How sure can we be that students are not faking their responses? Although we hope that serious student engagement will be evident in our assessments, we need to examine this element.

SOURCES OF VALIDITY EVIDENCE

Table 2.2 summarizes five types of evidence that can be used to evaluate the legitimacy of a validity claim. Different sources of evidence can, and often should, be used to support the same inference. The key is matching the right types of evidence with the intended inferences and uses.

Table 2.2   Summary of Sources of Evidence

Evidence Based On	Description
Test content or construct	Extent to which the assessment items represent a larger domain of interest or construct
Relations to other variables	High correlations with other measures of the same variable or criterion measures and low correlations with measures of related but different variables
Internal structure	Extent to which items measuring the same thing are correlated
Response processes and results	Consistency between hypothesized processes used and expected results with actual processes used and results
Consequences	Extent to which intended and unintended consequences of the assessment are appropriate and desired

Evidence Based on Test Content

The most important type of evidence in our current standards-based climate is based on the content of what is assessed. The idea is that the test items, when systematically reviewed, adequately measure the learning standard or objective. This evidence is used in two circumstances: (1) when there is a specific learning target or standard; and (2) when the test items represent a larger domain of knowledge, understanding, or skill.

It is difficult, if not impossible, to test students on everything they are taught or have learned. Typically, an identified *domain* represents the nature of what it is that we want to make an inference about. The domain, or universe, consists of all the knowledge, skills, or constructs of interest. What we do is assess a *sample* from the larger domain. Evidence based on test content (also referred to as content-related evidence or content validity) includes logical and empirical analyses of how well the sample in the assessment that is administered is representative of the larger domain.

For example, suppose a fifth-grade teacher is giving a unit test on insects, and the teacher intends to use the scores to show how much each student knows about everything that has been taught during the 6-week unit. Can you imagine how long the test would need to be to cover every fact, concept, and principle that students have been taught? The teacher must make some decisions to sample content from the entire domain and then use the scores on the sample items to make inferences about how much each student knows as defined in the larger domain. For example, if a student scores 75 percent correct on the test, the teacher infers that the student knows 75 percent of the content in the entire unit. How do you know if the teacher's decisions about the content to include in the test are such that the inference about the entire domain, which is made on the basis of the sample test items, is accurate? Here validity becomes a matter of professional judgment. In classroom assessment, the teacher usually makes a judgment about whether the sample is representative of the larger domain. This judgment process can be superficial or systematic. In a superficial review, the teacher makes the judgment in haste on the basis of appearance only. This is sometimes referred to as *face* validity. Face validity means that on a superficial review of the test, the content appears to be representative of the larger domain. While we clearly want to avoid poor face validity, more structured and systematic evidence is desirable.

In a similar way, test users make judgments about the nature of a construct that is being assessed by examining the items to determine if all aspects or components of the construct are represented in the appropriate degree. With constructs, we begin with a theoretical definition and rationale, then build the assessment to be consistent with that definition and rationale. This is important because of the abstract nature of construct. That is, there are different ways of conceptualizing a construct, none of which is necessarily better than others. Consider the construct "critical thinking." To examine critical thinking in education, you need a good match between what you want to emphasize in your school and the definition and theory represented in the particular measure you would like to use. Once the theory is consistent, an examination of the items is needed to make a judgment about how representative the items are with respect to the theoretical rationale.

Suppose a school decided to use a new student self-report instrument that was purportedly designed to identify students who are most at risk to fail and drop out of school. The instrument could be based on a theoretical model of resilience in which various factors contributing to resilience, such as having a hobby and a good relationship with an adult, were assessed. For use in a particular school, teachers would need to review the theoretical rationale and agree that it seemed reasonable for their students, then review the items to determine if the items were consistent with the theoretical rationale and weighted appropriately in the scoring.

Large-Scale Testing

In large-scale educational achievement testing, evidence based on test content begins with a detailed description of the content domain. Once the content domain is defined, items are developed and included in the test to represent the domain. These specifications, called *test blueprints* or *tables of specification*, will show the user and interpreter of the test the extent to which different content areas have been covered. An example of a test blueprint for the Virginia state testing program is illustrated in Table 2.3. In this example, state "Standards of Learning" (SOL) were used to indicate the content and skills to be covered on the tests. To establish strong evidence based on content, experts in the subject areas reviewed the tests and made systematic judgments about whether the items represented the content. These experts also made judgments about whether the percentage of items in different areas was appropriate and whether some areas that would be important were not on the test. With several individuals making such judgments, the review process is fairly systematic.

In the development of large-scale national standardized tests, the test developers will invest significant resources to be sure that appropriate knowledge and skills are assessed. For commercial test companies, who want their tests to be used in as many schools as possible, this process begins with suggestions from nationally recognized subject matter experts and, more recently, with content standards identified by national associations. Leading textbooks would also be examined to determine the domain of content and skills. Teachers and

Table 2.3   Example of Large-Scale Third-Grade Science Test Blueprint

Reporting Categories	No. of Items	Kindergarten SOLs	Grade 1 SOLs	Grade 2 SOLs	Grade 3 SOLs
Scientific investigation, reasoning, and logic	10	K.la-j K.2a, b	1.la-h	2.la-h	3.la-k
Force, motion, energy, and matter	10	K.3a, b K.4a-e K.5a-c	1.2a-d 1.3a-c	2.2a, b 2.3a, b	3.2a-c 3.3a-c
Life processes and living systems*	10	K.6a-c	1.4a-c 1.5a-c	2.4a, b 2.5a, b 2.7a 2.8a-c	3.4a, b 3.5a-c 3.6a-c 3.10a
Earth/space systems and cycles*	10	K.7a, b K.8a-d K.9a, b K.10a-c	1.6a, b 1.7a-c 1.8a-d	2.6a, b 2.7b	3.7a-d 3.8 a, b 3.9a-c 3.10b-d 3.1la-e

SOLs excluded from this test: No SOLs are excluded.

Total number of operational items: 40

**Field-test items: 10

Total number of items: 50

*Standards from these resource strands are incorporated as these reporting categories.

**These field-test items will *not* be used to compute students' scores on the test.

Note: SOLs stands for Standards of Learning. Numbers and letters in the table refer to specific standards. Reporting categories are test subscales. This test includes SOL for four grade levels.

college professors might be used to indicate the nature of key concepts, ideas, and skills. Following item generation, teachers may be used to examine each item and classify it according to categories of the subject domain and type of cognitive skill being assessed (e.g., recall knowledge or understanding).

Local Classroom Assessment

For classroom assessment, test blueprints are sometimes used to indicate what will be assessed as well as the nature of the learning that will be represented in the assessment. An example of such a test blueprint is shown in Table 2.4. It is a two-way grid in which items are classified by content area and by the cognitive level of the learning. Although making such a blueprint provides a systematic approach to evidence based on content, many teachers will conclude that, in practice, the time it takes to do this outweighs the benefits derived. An alternative is to build a complete set of the learning objectives or targets, showing the number of items and/or percentage of test devoted to each.

Table 2.4   Example of Classroom Assessment Test Blueprint

Topic Area	Cognitive Level of Learning			
	Knowledge	Understanding	Application	Total
Types of clouds	5	3	4	12
Types of fronts	5	2	4	11
High and low pressure	6	6	5	17
Wind	7	3	6	16
Total	23	14	19	56

Note: The number of items is shown in this blueprint. Percentages of items can also be used to provide an overview of what is emphasized in different areas.

To make judgments about their assessments, teachers need to have a clear understanding of the nature and structure of the discipline that is taught. They need to know what constitutes true understanding and what is most essential to developing appropriate breadth and depth of the discipline. To do this, it is helpful for teachers to discuss with others what constitutes essential understandings and principles, and to review assessments to make judgments about whether an assessment, when considered as a whole, reflects these understandings and principles. This process is enabled by making sure that the language used in describing cognitive complexity is accurate. Table 2.5 shows how this can be accomplished to show differences between knowledge, understanding, and application.

Finally, with performance assessments, teachers need to extend the essential meaning of validity to how performance is scored. That is, the nature of the scoring criteria needs to reflect important learning objectives. For example, if

Table 2.5   Cognitive Levels of Learning

Cognitive Level	Definition	Types	Key Verbs
Knowledge	Remembering something	Declarative Procedural Recognition Recall Facts Claims Elements Comprehension	Identifies Retrieves Knows Selects Names Defines Reproduces Classifies Recognizes Define
Understanding	Use of knowledge to ascribe meaning	Simple Deep Explanation Interpretation	Understands Converts Translates Discriminates Explains Interprets Infers Distinguishes Predicts Compares Justifies Illustrate
Application	Use of knowledge and understanding to reason and solve problems	Analysis Synthesis Transferability Critical thinking Problem solving Judgment Designing Constructing Testing Perspective	Analyzes Synthesizes Transfers Reasons Generalizes Contrasts Infers Creates Hypothesizes

students are to learn a science skill in which a series of steps needs to be performed, a task that asks students to show their work would help establish a valid inference about whether students have the skill. In addition, to help provide a more valid inference, the scoring of the answers would take into account which steps the students demonstrated and which steps the students did not, giving partial credit where appropriate. If the teacher simply marks each item as correct or incorrect, the total score may not indicate very well what degree of skill the student actually possesses. That is, if items are scored solely as right or wrong, it would be an invalid inference to conclude that the student who missed all the items possesses none of the skills.

Evidence Based on Instruction

Whether the concern is with content or construct evidence to establish validity, it is important in both large-scale and local classroom assessment to have evidence based on instruction (what could be called *instructional* validity). Instructional validity is concerned with the alignment between what is taught or what students have the opportunity to learn, and what is assessed. What is the match between what was taught and what was assessed? Have students had an appropriate opportunity to learn what was assessed? These questions are important because they relate directly to many of the inferences to be made.

Large-Scale Assessment

In large-scale assessment, the alignment between instruction and assessment is critical to high-stakes judgments about students, teachers, and schools.

Suppose a national norm-referenced achievement test is used to determine mathematics achievement. If the mathematics content in the test is not matched with what students have been taught, it would be unreasonable to conclude that the low scores mean that the school is not doing a good job. Similarly, it would not be valid to conclude that a school with low scores on a state competency exam is deficient or poor if the instruction provided does not match well with what is on the exam.

Local Classroom Assessment

For a classroom teacher, this essentially means asking the question, "Were the concepts actually taught, and taught well enough, so that students can perform well and demonstrate their understanding?" Often, this type of judgment is made just before an assessment is written in final form and administered because the answer can be known only after instruction has occurred. Although teachers may begin with an instructional plan, and even have an assessment instrument that is already prepared, only when most of the instruction is completed can the teacher determine for sure the match between what has been taught and emphasized and what is on the test. In making this determination, the teacher, one hopes, will also be able to conclude that student performance is due to learning and not to other factors such as the format of the assessment (e.g., some students are better with multiple-choice), gender, social desirability (e.g., pleasing the teacher when completing an attitude survey), and other influences that would lessen the validity.

Evidence Based on Relations to Other Variables

A second way to ensure appropriate inferences from assessment results is to have evidence that the scores are related to other variables in significant and predictable ways. There are two types of such evidence, one based on how a measure is related to other, external measures (test-criterion relationships) and one based on obtaining a pattern of relationships (convergent and discriminant evidence). Most of my emphasis will be on the first type.

Test-Criterion Relationships

One type of relationship occurs when a set of scores is correlated to another measure of the same content or construct or to some behavior or performance. This other measure, behavior, or performance is usually called a *criterion* measure. A correlation coefficient is calculated as a measure of the relationship and may be called the *validity coefficient*. Traditionally, there are two types of test-criterion relationships, *concurrent criterion-related* and *predictive criterion-related*. A concurrent coefficient indicates a relationship between two measures that are given at about the same time. A predictive criterion-related coefficient indicates how accurately test data can predict scores from a criterion measure that are gathered at a later time.

In establishing predictive evidence, there are many influences on the criterion measure, making a correlation difficult to establish. Consider the use of grades obtained in high school as a criterion measure for the SAT. Think for a moment about all the factors that affect student grades. Motivation, study skills, peer groups, work, family, effort, goals, and interpersonal skills are all important in determining grades, in addition to academic aptitude as measured by the SAT. Actually, student grades in high school are better predictors of college grades than any aptitude test because they tend to account for more factors. On the other hand, predictors that are almost the same as criterion measures (e.g., aptitude tests given at different ages) will result in a high correlation.

Given these influences, it is not surprising that the correlations typically reported as evidence based on predictive criterion-related relationships are moderate (e.g., .50 to .60). This means that the predictor measure can provide some degree of prediction, but it will be far from perfect. This is one reason why important placement decisions should never be made solely on the basis of a single test score. For instance, requiring students to take remedial summer school if they fail to achieve a designated "cut score" on a measure that purportedly predicts how well students will perform the following year is problematic because many factors contribute to student performance. The result achieved on the predictor test can represent only a part of the prediction.

Test-criterion evidence is used extensively by effective teachers by obtaining two or more measures of the same trait and looking for discrepancies between the scores. This is typically done informally though systematically. That is, the teacher knows what evidence is needed to corroborate the results of other assessments. Thus, teachers may see if homework results are consistent with in-class quizzes, or if observations of students working individually suggest the same level of understanding as evaluated by small group performance.

Teachers constantly make informal predictions of student learning, based on their observations of student work or answers to questions. With experience, effective teachers learn that certain types of behavior and student response will predict how well students will perform on tests. Once this relationship is established, it can be used to help future students obtain the assistance they need to succeed.

Convergent and Discriminant Evidence

Strong evidence for validity is demonstrated when certain patterns of correlations are reported for two or more measures or instruments. *Convergent* evidence is obtained when scores from one instrument correlate highly with scores from another measure of the same trait or performance (similar to concurrent criterion-related evidence). *Discriminant* evidence exists when scores from one instrument correlate poorly with scores from another measure of something different. When convergent correlations are high and the discriminant correlations are low, the pattern suggests strong evidence. For example, scores from a measure of self-concept would be expected to correlate highly with scores from a different but similar measure of self-concept but to show low correlation with related but different traits such as anxiety and motivation. The discriminant pattern can also be found by examining the subscales within a single instrument. For self-concept, for example, there are often different subscales (academic, social, and physical). Strong evidence for validity would exist if the subscales are not too highly correlated with each other.

Convergent and discriminant evidence is used extensively in developing psychological instruments that assess constructs such as self-concept, personality, attitudes, values, interests, and beliefs. An array of correlation coefficients is presented to show the predicted pattern of relationships.

In the classroom, teachers can apply the logic of this type of evidence by taking note of the consistency of student performance on different measures of the same knowledge or skill (convergent) and by seeing if there is less correlation with assessments of different knowledge or skills (discriminant). This is useful in identifying specific areas that need attention. For example, a teacher might use the following logic as evidence that an inference about a student's comprehension skills is valid: "Sam is able to read all types of different reading passages well in class and on standardized tests" (convergent evidence) "but doesn't always demonstrate a clear understanding of what he reads" (discriminant evidence). The inference is that Sam needs further instruction in comprehension. This conclusion would be less valid if based only on comprehension scores because there would be no evidence that the measure of comprehension was different from reading ability.

Evidence Based on Internal Structure

Large-Scale Assessment

Large-scale and standardized psychological assessments are usually designed so that several items are used to measure each separate trait or important reporting category. The item clusters are identified by how a construct is defined or by identified categories. For example, a measure of classroom climate would have several similar items that indicate a given theoretical dimension of climate, such as friendship or cohesiveness. If the items focusing on friendship are strongly related to each other and, at the same time, related less to items measuring other components, then there is good evidence based on internal structure. On the other hand, if the friendship items correlate highly with cohesion or goal orientation, or some other dimensions, then the evidence is weak, meaning that it may not be appropriate to report friendship as a separate aspect of classroom climate. Thus, evidence based on internal structure is provided when the relationships among items and parts of the instrument are empirically consistent with the construct, theory, or intended use of the scores.

Local Classroom Assessment

In the classroom, this type of evidence is typically used in criterion-referenced testing, albeit informally. Teachers use the combined results of several items that cover the same skill, concept, principle, or application. It is recommended that students need to answer a minimum of six to eight selected-response items to obtain sufficient consistency to conclude from the results that the students do or do not understand.

To illustrate, suppose a math teacher is constructing a unit geometry test. One of the skills to be assessed is the ability to determine the area of circles and cylinders. To obtain good evidence based on internal structure, the test needs to have several items that assess the ability of the students to determine area of circles and several items focused on cylinders. It wouldn't make much sense to give a two-item test—one item on circles and one on cylinders. Rather, several items for each are needed, and consistency in responses would provide good evidence for the validity of the inference that students do or do not know how to find the area of circles and cylinders.

Evidence Based on the Consequences of Assessments

In recent years, there has been considerable discussion among testing experts about whether the overall judgment of validity of uses and interpretations should include a consideration of the possible *consequences* of using the assessments (Messick, 1989, 1995; Popham, 1997; Shepard, 1997). Consequences could be both planned and unintended. For example, a desirable consequence of using essay questions may be that students learn the content with more depth of understanding than if they prepare for a multiple-choice test.

Large-Scale Assessment

For many large-scale tests, the implicit purpose is to have predetermined consequences, such as a placement test to determine which level of a foreign language the student should take, a high school graduation test to determine if a student is eligible to obtain a graduation certificate, and end-of-year course tests to screen students for summer school. Clearly, in all these cases, the use of the assessment involves important consequences.

The issue of evidence based on consequences takes on a different perspective when considering broader effects, social consequences, and usually negative, unintended effects. The current trend toward more and more "high-stakes" testing, in which large-scale assessments are used to deny grade promotion, high school graduation, and school accreditation, may result in several negative outcomes in the school, such as a narrowing of the curriculum so that it focuses on only the knowledge and skills measured. Important subjects that are not tested may be ignored. Drill-and-practice instructional activities may be used in excess to ensure that students score well, especially if the test emphasizes knowledge as opposed to reasoning. Suppose teachers become less creative and less spontaneous in response to high-stakes student testing. Will teachers change their classroom assessments to match the format used in a high-stakes test? If so, is this desirable? What is the long-term effect?

Local Classroom Assessment

On a more informal level, teachers use the concept of consequential validity continuously. For example, teachers may assess student understanding during instruction with some questions and use the results of the "assessment" to form small groups of students. The consequence is forming the small group of students, and the evidence comes in when the performance of the students is examined. If student performance is maximized, then there is evidence that the use of the informal assessment was valid. Or a teacher may decide, on the basis of informal assessment, that the entire class needs remediation before moving on in the textbook. The consequence is doing the remediation. The evidence is whether the remediation helped.

At the classroom level, student motivation and learning processes are often influenced by the nature of the assessment. A consequence of heavily using objective items is to encourage students to learn for recognition, whereas essay items motivate students to learn in a way that stresses the organization of information, principles, and application. An important effect of essay items is to engage students in reasoning skills, something that is much more difficult with objective items.

SUGGESTIONS FOR ENHANCING CLASSROOM ASSESSMENT VALIDITY

In large-scale testing, there are established procedures for obtaining correlation coefficients as validity evidence. In local classroom assessments, however, teachers must rely largely on nonstatistical procedures to establish the validity of their uses and inferences. Here is a list of suggestions for classroom teachers to enhance validity of their local assessment decisions and conclusions:

- Determine if different ways of assessing the same thing give similar results.
- Ask other teachers to review your assessment for clarity and purpose.

- Make sure to sample the performance or behavior several times. Don't rely on a single measure.
- Prepare a blueprint, and, prior to testing, share it with your students.
- Ask other teachers to judge the match between the assessment and learning objectives.
- Compare one group of students who are expected to obtain high scores with students of another group who are expected to obtain low scores.
- Compare scores obtained before instruction with scores obtained after instruction.
- Compare predicted, intended consequences with actual consequences.
- Use different methods to measure the same learning objective.

Validity lies at the heart of teacher decision making by establishing guidelines and procedures for determining the quality of the decisions. Validity is also critical to the appropriate use of standardized, large-scale assessment results. The next chapter shows how another characteristic of assessment, reliability, is a necessary but not sufficient aspect of scores for making reasonable validity claims.

3

Reliability

Like validity, the term *reliability* describes an essential characteristic of high-quality assessment. Indeed, the assessment process must provide reliable scores as a necessary condition for validity. Also like validity, reliability is a conclusion based on evidence that is gathered in a variety of ways, and there are clear differences between reliability for local classroom assessments and reliability for large-scale assessments.

WHAT IS RELIABILITY?

Reliability is concerned with the consistency of scores obtained from assessment. It can be more formally defined as the extent to which assessment scores are dependable and free from error. Notice that this definition stresses the consistency of *scores*, not tests or instruments. This point is important because reliability, like validity, is a judgment about the scores obtained from a specific instance in which students were required to respond to questions. The scores, not the test, are reliable.

The emphasis on the reliability of scores, and not of tests themselves, is critical to a complete understanding of reliability. Reliability is not a test characteristic that accompanies the test wherever and whenever it is given because a score that is obtained is influenced by many more factors than the nature or quality of the test. Consequently, to understand the results, you must also understand the factors that may affect the scores. So, although you may hear or read something about "the reliability of the *test*," remember that it really refers to the reliability of the *scores.*

Table 3.1 illustrates the concept of reliability with two sets of scores. Two 20-question quizzes are used to assess second graders' addition and subtraction

35

skills at different times. The same addition and subtraction test is used each time. If the scores are reliable, there will be a high degree of consistency between the two sets of scores that measure either addition or subtraction. In this example, the addition scores are consistent, pretty much the same from one time to the next time, which indicates high reliability. In contrast, there is little consistency in the results obtained for the subtraction quiz. What does this mean? Because the goal is to have a good estimate of the students' level of skills, the consistency of the scores on the addition quiz allows the test user to make reasonable inferences (e.g., Deon has much stronger addition skills than does Mary). The inconsistent results on the subtraction quizzes, however, mean that these scores should not be used to make inferences about the subtraction skills of the students. More subtraction assessments that yield more dependable results would be needed to establish reliability.

Table 3.1   Student Performance on Quizzes (Number Correct) to Illustrate Reliability

Student	Addition		Subtraction	
	Quiz 1	Quiz 2	Quiz 1	Quiz 2
Felix	15	16	12	18
Ryan	12	13	19	11
Rob	19	18	20	14
Deon	18	18	13	19
Mary	10	11	9	20

Here is another example to illustrate the meaning of reliability. Think about the difference between a measure of self-concept and a measure of the time taken to complete a sailboat race (number of hours, minutes, and seconds). The measure of self-concept will have relatively low consistency because so many factors affect how an individual responds to questions about self-concept, such as the person's mood that day, recent experiences, time of day, heat in the room, degree of fatigue, what the person was told about the survey, and so on. The measure of time, on the other hand, provides a reliable result—a precise, dependable indication of time with little possible error. Even with a measure of time, however, there is some degree of error, such as the dependability of the watch and the ability of the timekeeper to press stop or start appropriately.

Reliability and validity are easily confused because both are concerned with scores and not instruments and because the language seems similar (valid inferences are accurate; reliable scores are dependable). To help, think of the difference in this way: Reliability addresses whether scores are consistent, whereas validity concerns the nature and meaning of the scores. For example, a measure of the circumference of each student's wrist will provide a reliable result, but it would be absurd to use the scores to indicate reading ability. Likewise, a multiple-choice computer literacy test may provide reliable scores (students get about the same score each time they take the test), but it may not be valid to infer that the students who obtain high scores have stronger computer application skills than students who obtain low scores. Figure 3.1 provides an additional illustration of the relationship between validity and reliability. Think of the target as a learning objective, with the center being the essence of what needs to be assessed. It shows how a score can be highly reliable (scores from Target 3) yet at the same time invalid.

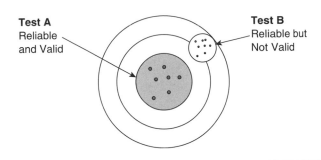

Figure 3.1   Illustration of Reliability and Validity

HOW IS RELIABILITY DETERMINED?

Reliability is determined by estimating the amount of error that accompanies the obtained score. If there is little error, then the reliability is high. If there is much error, the reliability is low. How, then, do we go about estimating the degree of error? It is helpful to consider two major sources of error, those rooted in the students, called internal, and those that are external to the students. Internal factors include those that can vary from one time to another or from one situation to another but reside within the person. For instance, each of us knows how our moods can change and affect our performance. We can have the same knowledge but test poorly on one day because we are sick and score high another day, in part, because we feel sharp. External factors include influences that are outside the person, such as differences among testing sites regarding the distractions students must put up with, test question ambiguity, random error, and differences attributed to scorer subjectivity.

Internal and external sources of error are illustrated in Figure 3.2, which shows how they are combined to influence the observed score or result. Think about three sources of influence that determine the observed score: the actual knowledge or skill of the student, internal factors, and external factors.

It would be nice if assessment results were dependent solely on students' knowledge or skill, but that simply doesn't happen with a single test or performance. There is *always* some degree of internal and/or external error contributing to the observed score. Reliability helps estimate the amount of internal and external error, but most traditional reliability procedures *underestimate* the actual amount of error. In other words, there is typically more error than may

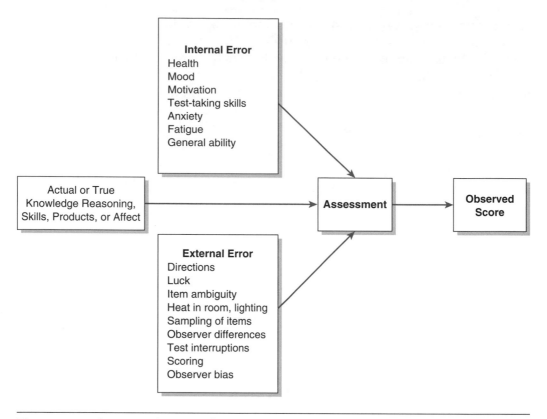

Figure 3.2   Sources of Error Influencing Reliability

Source: Adapted from McMillan, J. H. (2007). *Classroom Assessment: Principles and Practice for Effective Standards-Based Instruction* (4th ed.). Boston: Allyn & Bacon. Copyright © Allyn & Bacon. Used with permission.

be reported by reliability data. This is especially true for newer forms of assessment that use scorer judgments to make ratings of performance. The potency of any single error factor depends on the testing situation, nature of the assessment, scoring, and how scores are interpreted. A particular factor, such as conditions of the room, can have a major impact on scores in one assessment but have a minor influence on another assessment.

Reliability is determined by estimating the influence of various sources of error. In large-scale testing, the process is formalized by calculating correlations and reporting the correlations as reliability coefficients. In classroom assessment, there is rarely any statistical estimate of reliability, although software programs make this quite easy. Rather, in classrooms, teachers informally notice some sources of error and take them into account when interpreting results. For example, if Ms. Lopez knows that Susan is distracted by a family problem and simply doesn't concentrate on the test, she can conclude that Susan's low score is heavily influenced by this external factor. In other words, the observed score has considerable error. The reliability of the assessment *for Susan* is weak. It could be strong for other students.

In the next section, different types of reliability estimates are summarized. While these approaches are formalized in large-scale and other standardized assessments, the logic of each is important for classroom assessment.

SOURCES OF RELIABILITY EVIDENCE

Evidence Based on Stability

A stability estimate of reliability refers to consistency over time. The stability of scores is estimated by administering an assessment to a group of individuals, waiting for a specified time (typically a week or more), and then re-administering the same assessment to the same group of individuals. The correlation between the two sets of scores is then calculated to obtain a statistical indication of the reliability. This type of estimate is also called *test-retest* reliability. The example of test scores in Table 3.1 is an example of two informal stability estimates. If the performance is about the same on the second test as it was on the first test, as was true for addition in Table 3.1, then the reliability is high. But if the results look like those for the subtraction tests in Table 3.1, the stability and reliability of the scores are both low.

Large-Scale Assessment

Stability estimates constitute good evidence for reliability in large-scale assessment when the trait or performance that is assessed is not expected to change during the time span between the assessments. For this reason, stability estimates are not typically used for psychological assessments that measure traits that are expected to change, such as mood and perception. Also, many psychological instruments (as well as some measures of achievement) are *reactive*, allowing that persons taking the assessment once may change simply because of the experience of taking it. With large-scale achievement tests, students may change their performance because of practice and/or memory. In measuring abilities, such as reading comprehension, change would be hoped for during the long term, but during a short time span, the scores would be expected to be stable. Because aptitude test scores are used to make inferences about future behavior or performance, stability evidence needs to be collected. An example would be a readiness test that measures aptitudes and abilities with the purpose of predicting success. These scores would be much less useful if there wasn't some assurance that the aptitudes and abilities are stable between the time tested and time of placement.

Stability estimates are often low because of the number of factors that can affect the scores. One way to think about it is to examine the internal and external sources of error in Figure 3.2 and see how these could vary from one instance to another. Time becomes a critical factor that influences the correlation. There will be an inverse relationship between the time span between two administration times and the strength of the correlation. That is, as the time interval increases, the correlation decreases.

Local Classroom Assessment

In general, stability estimates in the form of correlation coefficients will not be used in classroom assessment. But teachers will benefit from using the logic of stability in evaluating student work. When performances should be stable, an informal review of the results, by comparing scores or ranks, will provide some evidence of reliability. Another approach is for teachers to examine the consistency of decisions made about students over time. For example, a teacher may use an assessment to place students in cooperative groups. On the basis of the test scores, students may be placed into one of three groups—high, medium, and low. From a stability standpoint for reliability, the teacher could use the same assessment again and determine the percentage of students classified the same way on both assessments. Here the focus is not on the specific scores but on the decision. If most or even many of the students are classified differently the second time, then the assessment would not be reliable. As we will see, decision-oriented evidence also plays a major role in providing reliability data for criterion-referenced assessments.

Evidence Based on Equivalent Forms

An estimate of equivalence is obtained by administering two forms of the same assessment to a group of students and correlating the scores. This type of evidence may be called *alternate* or *parallel form* reliability. The approach is to generate two forms of an assessment that are equal in what is being measured. If the two forms are given at approximately the same time (same day or week), then an estimate of only equivalence is obtained. If there is a significant time delay between the administrations, then a stability feature is added, providing an estimate of equivalence *and* stability.

Large-Scale Assessment

Equivalent forms evidence is used extensively in standardized testing and high-stakes testing in which students need to pass tests to advance in grade or graduate from high school. Several forms of the same test are needed to allow retakes and makeup testing. If tests are used in this way, evidence based on equivalence is essential. A relatively new procedure, called *item response theory*, is often used with standardized tests to establish reliable scores on tests that invariably differ somewhat with respect to difficulty.

Local Classroom Assessment

In classroom assessment, teachers rarely use formal equivalence evidence because it would be unusual to have to generate more than a single form of each assessment. But equivalence is a factor if students are offered makeup tests or if teachers want to use different forms in a pretest-posttest research design. The difficulty for teachers is knowing when two forms are "equivalent."

Evidence Based on Internal Consistency

Internal consistency evidence is based on the degree of homogeneity of the items that measure the same trait. Unlike for stability and equivalence, only a single administration of an assessment is needed. The logic is that if many items measure the same thing, scores based on these items should be correlated with each other. For example, a teacher would expect a student who has clearly mastered knowledge of the parts of a flower to get most or all items correct on a 10-question test. In contrast, a student who knew nothing about the parts of flowers would be expected to get most of or all of the ten items wrong. In other words, internal consistency estimates how well items within an assessment are functioning in a consistent manner.

Large-Scale Assessment

There are three common types of internal consistency estimates that are used with large-scale assessments: *split-half, Kuder-Richardson,* and *coefficient alpha.* In the split-half method, the test items are typically divided into "equal" halves by whether the items are even numbered or odd numbered; then each half is scored separately for each student. The total scores for each of the halves are correlated to provide a reliability coefficient. This approach works fine for tests that have ten or more items measuring the same trait.

The Kuder-Richardson formulas (KR 20, KR 21) are used for tests in which each item is scored dichotomously (e.g., right or wrong). You can think of the KR approaches as the average of correlating the totals from all possible halves of the test. This avoids the problem of having to determine how to separate the scores to obtain equal halves. When assessments are scored using a scale that has more than two levels, such as what is commonly found in attitude surveys (e.g., using a scale such as *strongly agree, agree, disagree, strongly disagree*), coefficient alpha is used to generate a reliability coefficient.

The use of internal consistency estimates is widespread. From a practical standpoint, internal consistency evidence is relatively easy to establish. There is no need to develop a second form, nor is it necessary to give the assessment more than once. There is one important limitation, however—there needs to be a sufficient number of items. The rule of thumb is that at least five items are needed to measure each separate trait or skill. This is very important for using results reported by individual item, or by two or three items.

Local Classroom Assessment

When teachers build an achievement test, there are typically many items that measure a single trait. This is what occurs when there is a unit test and a total score is obtained. The logic of internal consistency means that reliability is based on a single estimate at only one point in time. This is an important consideration in classroom tests because teachers want to know that students can demonstrate a skill or can show their understanding from day to day or week to week. We want students to remember what they have learned. If the only estimate we have is internal consistency data, the best we can conclude is that students were able to demonstrate understanding and skill *at that particular time.* Changes in the person from day to day would not be accounted for. In other words, internal consistency estimates alone will underestimate the actual amount of error that should be considered in interpreting the scores.

Evidence Based on Scorer or Rater Consistency

Whenever student responses need to be judged, rated, or scored, an additional source of error is introduced that may be important. Examples of these types of assessments include grading essays, scoring writing samples, evaluating performance assessments and portfolios, and grading papers and projects. In each case, someone, usually the classroom teacher, has to review and evaluate the work, and in this evaluation process, additional error is introduced. These errors include biases of the scorer; the halo effect (evaluating on the basis of a general impression of the student, e.g., "Sally is a good student; this answer is good"); fatigue; general expectations; and other idiosyncrasies of the scorer.

Large-Scale Assessment

Two approaches are typically used to establish reliability evidence based on scorer or rater consistency in large-scale assessment: a percentage agreement approach and a correlational approach. The percentage agreement method typically uses simple agreement among two or more raters or agreement within one or more points. It is obtained by asking two or more scorers or raters to judge the same set of student performances. The number of exact matches can be added and then divided by the total number of judgments to get a percentage that indicates consistency. Suppose, for example, two teachers independently rate a set of 20 student portfolios on a scale of 1 to 6. The results are summarized in Table 3.2. The number of exact matches is 15, which results in an agreement index of 75 percent, which is very good. This indicates that error attributed to the scorer is not great.

If agreement within one point is used, then 19 of the 20 scores would be used to calculate the percentage, now 95 percent. It is obvious that if you loosen the criteria for what determines a "match," the percentage agreement is going to go up. How do you know which to use, the exact match or matching within one or possibly more points? The answer depends on a number of factors. The first factor is the nature of the scale or rating. If you use more points on a scale, then it makes sense to use matching within one or more points. For example, if teachers were grading essays and gave each one up to 50 points, it might be reasonable to think of a match as within 5 points. On the other hand, if the judgment is into one of three categories, it would be best to use exact matches. The second factor is the description of various points on the scale and the relative distinction between them. Consider the following scoring rubric for language:

1 Inadequate	2 Minimal	3 Adequate	4 Superior
Grammar and vocabulary very poor	Many grammar mistakes; simplistic language	Few grammar mistakes; appropriate language	Excellent grammar and language

Table 3.2   Portfolio Scores Assigned by Different Teachers

	Score	
Student	Teacher 1	Teacher 2
Mehdi	5	5
Suzanne	2	3
Angie	5	5
Daisy	6	6
Reed	4	5
Stephen	2	2
Maike	3	3
Pat	1	2
Robert	5	5
Jon	4	4
Faye	4	4
George	3	5
Kim	6	6
Jim	5	5
Kristin	2	2
Diona	4	4
Joel	1	1
Chuck	3	3
David	2	2
Barney	5	4

The degree of error with such a scale will probably be high because the criteria listed are vague, without much degree of specificity or clarity that would allow assigning each example a proper score. In the following scale, the criteria are much more detailed and would lead to a higher percentage of agreement.

1 Inadequate	2 Minimal	3 Adequate	4 Superior
Grammar and vocabulary so poor that most of the message is not understood	Grammar and vocabulary weak but allow understanding; many grammar mistakes; simplistic language	Grammar and vocabulary complex with few mistakes; language not overly simplistic	Excellent grammar and vocabulary, with only minor mistakes; language uses a variety of techniques such as humor, imagery, and metaphor

A final factor to consider is the training of the scorers. The expectation is that scorers or raters who are trained will achieve a higher rate of agreement than those not trained. In the training, it is important for the scorers to see many examples of completed products that align with different points on the scale. These examples are sometimes called anchors or benchmarks. Another consideration is to help scorers understand why a particular judgment is incorrect, providing additional practice until a high rate of agreement is achieved.

A second method of determining scorer or rater agreement is to calculate a correlation coefficient. With two scorers and a set of scores, such a correlation indicates the strength of agreement between the scorers. For the data from Table 3.2, the correlation is .92, which is very high.

An additional caution about scorer or rater agreement is that method does not take into consideration error attributed to the tasks, time, or sampling. Usually, only selected tasks are used, and these tasks are only one way to represent the problem or provide opportunities for students to demonstrate their knowledge or skill. A good example of this in large-scale assessment is the use of writing prompts when assessing students' writing and language skills. It is clear that some students are better able to respond to certain prompts that others would have difficulty with because of background and interests. So, the choice of a prompt is important. If prompts and performance tasks are not selected carefully, they can contribute to a weak generalization to the larger set of prompts or tasks that could be used in the assessment.

Local Classroom Assessment

Inter-rater reliability can be used extensively, in informal ways, by classroom teachers. While there would not be statistical estimates of agreement, as in large-scale assessments, teachers can easily ask other teachers in their building to review an answer with the established criteria, to see if there is agreement. This wouldn't need to be done for all students. Just a small sample of different levels of performance would suffice. This is especially helpful for beginning teachers.

A second kind of inter-rater reliability for classroom teachers is to see if more than one rater agrees about what is observed in the classroom. Two observers would need to be in the classroom at one time (the teacher of the class could be one observer). In comparing notes about what occurred, a consensus indicates good reliability. This approach can also be used to train individuals who will observe beginning teachers.

Table 3.3 summarizes the four sources of evidence that have been discussed. Keep in mind that even if correlations and percentage agreement are not formally calculated, the logic and type of consistency assessed are unique to each source and should match the nature of the inference you wish to draw from the scores.

RELIABILITY FOR STANDARDS-BASED INTERPRETATIONS

Much of the early work on reliability was based on tests for which norm-referenced inferences were made. The nature of the tests fit well with obtaining high correlations. But to make standards-based inferences, as is common in the classroom as well as large-scale assessment, the nature of the inference as pass/fail, novice/proficient/advanced, or other categorical decisions suggests a somewhat different approach to reliability. In addition, by their very nature, assessments used for standards-based interpretations often give a restricted range of scores. In the classroom, for example, test scores are usually pretty high with only a few low ones. Large-scale assessments, on the other hand, provide a set

Table 3.3   Sources of Evidence in Estimating Reliability

Source of Evidence	Description
Evidence based on stability (test-retest)	Estimates consistency of scores from two administrations of the same assessment to the same individuals with a time interval between the assessments
Evidence based on equivalent forms	Estimates consistency of scores obtained from two forms of the same assessment, given at the same time or with a time interval (equivalence and stability)
Evidence based on internal consistency	Estimates consistency of scores measuring the same trait obtained from a single administration of the assessment
Evidence based on scorer or rater consistency	Estimates consistency of scores by calculating the agreement between two or more scorers or raters of the same performances

of scores highly spread out along the possible range of results. This occurs whether the large-scale assessment is norm-referenced or standards-based.

The basic approach for obtaining evidence of reliability for standards-based interpretations is to focus on the decision or classification, and to examine the consistency of making similar decisions or classifications. For example, if a test is designed to classify students as masters or nonmasters, a "cut" score will be established to make the decision for each student. Without dwelling on the methods of establishing such cut scores, let's suppose this was done in a reasonable fashion. Consistency is obtained by examining what percentages of the classifications are the same on two administrations of the same test, on different forms of the same test, or on a single administration (similar to internal consistency). Suppose a group of 20 students took the same test twice. On the first administration, 10 were classified as masters, and 10 as nonmasters. Of the 10 classified as masters on the first administration, 8 were classified this way on the second administration. All 10 students initially classified as nonmasters were also classified nonmasters on the second test. So of all the 20 classifications, there were matches with 18. That is, 18 of the 20 students were classified the same way. This can be converted to a percentage—90 percent in this case.

For those who like formulas for this type of thinking, the following will work when there is a dichotomous classification:

% Consistency = (Number classified master both times + Number classified nonmaster both times)/Total number in the group.

You may be wondering how high the percentage needs to be to conclude that the inference about mastery is reasonably reliable. To answer this question, you need to compare the percentage obtained to what could have been achieved by chance. For example, in a dichotomous classification, if you did the sorting randomly, you would find 50 percent consistency. So, a result not much beyond 50 percent indicates poor reliability. At the other extreme, finding 90 percent consistency suggests that the inference is reliable. When you have more than two classifications, as is the case for many performance and portfolio assessments, the chance percentage is less. Because there is also greater opportunity for misclassification, however, acceptable percentages range from 70 to 85 percent.

Another element in interpreting the percentage consistently classified concerns the nature of the decision to be made. When standards-based interpretations are used to determine eligibility for graduation or other high-stakes decisions, the standard for reliability needs to be high. Less stringent standards are needed for decisions that do not have important long-term consequences, such as deciding whether to review a given topic for a final exam. For important decisions, there should be several opportunities for students to demonstrate the needed level of competency. A useful way to think about reliability in such situations is to estimate the percentage of students misclassified after several opportunities. The logic in multiple opportunities is that through time, other sources of error can be accounted for. For instance, if a student is not feeling well the first time and fails, the next time provides an opportunity to show what can be done when the student is feeling better.

FACTORS INFLUENCING RELIABILITY ESTIMATES

Several factors influence reliability, either the magnitude of statistical reliability estimates that are obtained for large-scale or less formal judgments about classroom assessments.

Spread of Scores

Reliability coefficients are directly related to the degree of spread of the scores that are used in the calculations. Other things being equal, the greater the spread of scores, the higher the reliability. In other words, if the assessment results in a large range of scores, a higher correlation may be obtained. A greater spread results if the group being assessed has a range of scores. This has implications when assessing a group of students who are fairly homogeneous with respect to the trait being assessed (e.g., an honors-level class). Because the students achieve at the same high level, there is a low range of scores.

The ideal spread of scores for making standards-based decisions is illustrated in Figure 3.3a. Because there is little overlap between the "masters" and "nonmasters" groups, the decision for each student is reliable. In contrast, in Figure 3.3b you have a lot of overlap between the two groups, so the decisions are much less reliable. Think about this when setting a "cut" score for standards-based decisions. If the results show a normal distribution (as is typically achieved in all large-scale testing), then drawing a line at, say, the 60th percentile means that quite a few students are so close to the cut point that many of these will be misclassified (see Figure 3.4).

(a)

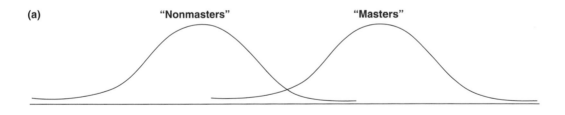

Figure 3.3a   Distributions Resulting in Reliable Decisions

(b)

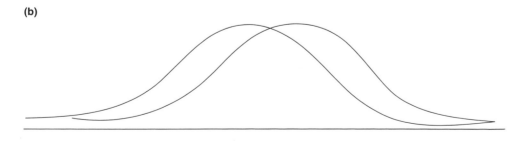

Figure 3.3b   Distributions Resulting in Unreliable Decisions

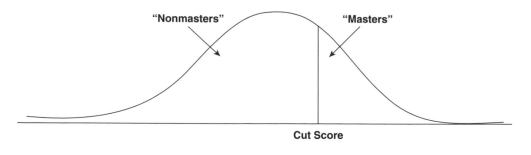

Figure 3.4   Standards-Based Cut Score Reliability

Number of Items

Generally, the more items of the same trait, the higher the reliability will be. This is because a longer assessment with many items does a better job of sampling the trait or behavior. Also, the error associated with specific items has less influence on a longer assessment. Imagine giving students a single mathematics problem to assess their ability to multiply fractions. The scores and resulting inferences about student ability would be highly unreliable. Students would get either a 100 or a 0 on the "test." But what if the item selected was a relatively difficult one? Students who may have been able to answer less difficult items do not have an opportunity to demonstrate their actual ability levels. Finally, having more items on objective tests lessens the influence of guessing on the total score.

Keep in mind that the number of similar independent items or tasks, not simply the length of the assessment, is important in enhancing reliability. Thus, several shorter assessments usually provide a more reliable result than one or two long assessments. Teachers, by and large, are more interested in the reliability of the decision, grade, or final outcome than in a single assessment, so, from a practical standpoint, the principle of more assessment tasks for good reliability is important.

Difficulty of Assessment Items

Here is one of my favorite examples of test item difficulty. Is there a difference in the difficulty level of the following items that assess the same knowledge?

Which of the following is the state capital of Michigan?

a. Miami

b. New York

c. Lansing

d. Atlanta

> Which of the following is the state capital of Michigan?
>
> a. Grand Rapids
>
> b. Detroit
>
> c. Ann Arbor
>
> d. Lansing

Obviously, the ability of a student to get the correct answer is a function of the difficulty of the items. If all the items are very easy or very hard, traditional reliability indexes will be low. High reliability correlations are obtained when there is a mix of difficulty in the items, with most ranging from 40 to 70 percent of the students obtaining correct answers. At least, this is typical for large-scale assessments. In the classroom, teachers typically build tests that are much easier. It does make sense to err on the side of leniency because teachers want to provide students a fair opportunity to show what they know and can do. Also, very difficult tests encourage guessing, which lowers reliability.

Quality of Assessment Items and Tasks

Naturally, the quality of the items and tasks is important for reliability. If the items are poorly worded, are misleading, have poor distracters, or do not discriminate well between known masters and nonmasters, then reliability will suffer. Because teachers do not usually pretest items, they determine that there is a problem *after* the assessment has been completed. At this point, it is fine to eliminate problematic items and rescore the assessment for all the students (even if that means working with a total score other than 10, 20, 25, 50, or 100!). Once the scoring is complete, teachers can do an item analysis to determine which items will need to be revised for the future. Performance assessment tasks also need to be evaluated after students' responses have been recorded to get an indication of the quality of the task.

Objectivity in Scoring

Objectivity in assessment can refer either to the nature of the item (e.g., selected-response, such as multiple-choice) or to the nature of the scoring. Here, the interest is in the degree of objectivity in the scoring procedures. With objective items, this is clear because the scoring is highly objective and has little error. Constructed-response items, such as essays, papers, projects, and performance assessments, are subject to different degrees of scoring error, depending on the nature of the question and the scoring procedures. Fill-in-the-blank constructed-response items are scored fairly objectively, with little scorer error expected. Student responses and products that are subject to greater scorer bias, however, can have a detrimental effect on reliability.

Differences Among Individuals Assessed

Just as traditional reliability indices depend on a good spread of scores, they also depend on having a group that has a spread of knowledge, ability, or skill being assessed. That is, if everyone who is assessed has the same knowledge, ability, or skill level, a reliability correlation coefficient based on that group will be low. This principle poses a difficulty for teachers who are striving to get all students to a mastery level, so examining the reliability of the decision is more appropriate. In this case, reliability of the decision is helpful. Even then, however, if all students show mastery, there is insufficient information to determine what was not known or demonstrated. This principle helps explain why large-scale tests typically report "stronger" reliability than classroom tests. Large-scale test development includes a more heterogeneous sample of students than is typically found in the classroom.

STANDARD ERROR OF MEASUREMENT

I would be remiss if I did not address *standard error of measurement* (SEM) in this chapter. As you recall, reliability is all about error. The SEM is a statistical way to indicate the magnitude of the error. Although, as test users, we know that error is present in every educational assessment, we are able to estimate error only on the basis of observed results of an assessment. We never know for sure what type or amount of error has actually influenced each observed score. Therefore, we *estimate* the margin of error that is probable, given the reliability of the test and the spread of scores, and call it SEM.

A useful way to think about SEM is to imagine what would happen if a student took the same test over and over again. Because of error, the scores received would not be the same. Suppose the obtained scores were 75, 78, 72, 74, and 75. Which one of these would be closest to the real knowledge or skill of the student? We can't know for sure. But we *do* know that the student's real knowledge or skill is probably between 72 and 78. It could even be reported as 75 + or − 3. While the actual calculation of SEM is precise, this illustration provides a way to think about the principle conceptually.

PRACTICAL SUGGESTIONS FOR CLASSROOM ASSESSMENT

So what does all this have to say to teachers who need some practical guidelines to improve the reliability of their assessments? One reality is that teachers give many assessments that, although individually may not have established reliability evidence, when totaled at the end of the unit or semester these assessments can result in a reliable overall judgment. Given that most teachers will not be calculating correlations, the following suggestions will be of benefit:

- Motivate students to put forth their best effort on assessments.
- Use a sufficient number of items or tasks. A minimum of five items is needed to assess a single trait or skill.
- Construct items, scoring criteria, and tasks that clearly differentiate students on what is being assessed, and make the criteria public.
- Make sure procedures for scoring constructed-response items are consistently applied to all students.
- Use independent raters or observers to score a sample of student responses, and check consistency with your evaluations.
- Build in as much objectivity in the scoring as possible and still maintain the integrity of what is being assessed.
- Continue assessments until the results are consistent.
- Eliminate or reduce external sources of error.
- Use shorter assessments more frequently than fewer long assessments.
- Use several types of assessment tasks or methods of assessment.
- Use clearly identified anchors and other examples to illustrate scoring criteria.
- To the extent possible, standardize assessment and scoring protocols and procedures.
- Keep an item and task bank or file; don't release tests to students for them to keep.

The most important aspect of reliability to keep in mind when designing and interpreting educational assessments is that error, to some degree, is part of every score. The goal is to understand the nature and extent of this error and then include this information when using the scores for instructional decision making, grades, and curriculum evaluation.

4

Fairness

The goal of assessment is to obtain a sound inference about what a student knows, understands, and can do. Such inferences can then lead to good decisions that enhance student learning and can also inform teachers, the public, and policy makers. While the principles of reliability and validity have served us well as the foundation of sound assessment, it has recently become evident that issues of fairness are equally important.

There are many ways to think about fairness in relation to educational assessment, and it is not possible to discuss all these complex issues in this book. A full consideration would explore testing in relation to broader social goals, and legal and ethical issues. I will be concerned with fairness as reflected in the nature of assessments and the use of information generated from assessments in classrooms and schools.

WHAT IS FAIRNESS?

The term *fairness* can be defined from several perspectives (Heubert & Hauser, 1999). It can be defined broadly as a condition or situation in which assessments are not unduly influenced by factors unrelated to the learning objectives or standards that are being measured. Fairness can also be described as equitable and just treatment of those being assessed. The term *bias* is often thought of as the opposite of fairness. Obviously, assessments should be free from bias, whether that bias is based on gender, race, socioeconomic status (SES), or other characteristics that may influence the performance being assessed. If some students have an advantage because of factors unrelated to what is being assessed, then the assessment is not fair.

Fair assessments are unbiased and nondiscriminatory, uninfluenced by irrelevant factors such as gender or race and by subjective factors such as the bias of a scorer. In other words, in a fair assessment, students have the opportunity to demonstrate their learning in a way such that their performance is not distorted by their race, gender, ethnic background, disability, or other factors unrelated to the purpose of the assessment. A fair assessment is also characterized by scoring that is not affected by these factors.

Unfair assessments result in performances that both underestimate and overestimate the traits being measured. A common example of unfair assessment is when particular groups of examinees are put at a disadvantage. This frequently occurs when there is something about the content of the assessment that makes it more difficult for students with certain characteristics. For example, suppose a test is designed to assess students' writing skills by asking them to respond to the following prompt:

> Write a short story about a boy who practices very hard to be good in basketball and makes the team.

This type of prompt may be easier for boys to respond to than for girls. Girls may score lower than boys not because they don't have the writing skills but because they are less familiar with this sport. This suggests that the prompt is biased against girls. On the other hand, boys may score higher because they have experience to draw from in writing their short stories. In either case, there is some distortion in the performance caused by a factor unrelated to what is being assessed. Another good example is a reading comprehension assessment in which the content of the reading passage favors one group over another. If the content is about a sailing experience, then examinees who live in a community in which sailing is ubiquitous would probably have an easier time reading and understanding the passage than would examinees who know little about sailing.

Although it is impossible to completely remove all unfair aspects of an assessment for every student, teachers and administrators can do much to ensure that assessments are as fair as possible. We can also understand the various ways fairness can affect our interpretations and uses of assessment results. This is particularly important given the increasingly diverse characteristics of students and increased emphasis on identification of students with special needs. Because of these conditions, fairness is just as important as the standbys of validity and reliability.

FAIRNESS RELATED TO STUDENT KNOWLEDGE OF LEARNING TARGETS AND ASSESSMENTS

Have you ever taken a test and then thought, "If I had known the test was going to cover this content, I would have studied it"? I know I have. A fair assessment is one in which it is clear to students what will and will not be tested, what test format will be used, and how the test will be scored. The goal is not to trick, fool, or outguess students about what is assessed. Rather, teachers need to be clear and relatively specific about the nature of the target students need to learn and how that performance will be scored. When this is communicated to all students *prior to instruction* and in a *public way*, students, as well as parents, know what needs to be learned. This approach helps students know what to study and focus on as well as how to study. For example, if students know that they will need to show their work on a mathematics test, they will practice showing their work and, it is hoped, receive feedback about what they show. If students know that they will have an essay test that will be graded with a known set of scoring criteria, they will pull together their thoughts in a way that organizes the content to respond to the criteria, rather than simply memorizing content.

Let's look at another example in more depth to illustrate the importance of specificity and clarity in learning targets, the test itself, and scoring criteria. Suppose you are going to teach a unit on cultural diversity. Here is the first learning target you identify:

Students will be able to identify and learn about different cultures.

You tell students that they will be tested on this learning target at the end of the unit. This information, although shared with students, is so general and vague that it indicates little about what will be learned, the test format, and the scoring criteria. Students are left guessing about what they really need to learn, what will be on the test, how they will be tested, and how the test will be scored. Consider the next more specific target and description of assessment:

Students will identify characteristics of several cultures and be able to show how they are both similar and different.

You inform students that the assessment will be a constructed-response test in which students will list the characteristics of each of the cultures and indicate ways they are similar and ways they are different. With this information, students have a much better idea about what to learn and how their learning will be assessed. There is much less guessing based on idiosyncratic student differences, which makes the assessment fairer.

Here, the target is even more specific:

Students will identify six characteristics of three cultures, explain how each culture differs from the others, and explain the implications of these differences and similarities on freedom of expression and tolerance.

Now students have a clear idea what they will learn and how they will be required to demonstrate their learning. This type of target is fairer because it takes the ambiguity out of the process, replacing it with clarity and specificity.

Another good illustration of the importance of the targets is learning to drive. Students take a driver education course with the expectation that certain specific skills will be tested. It would be unfair if students were taught to drive using an automatic transmission and then, when asked to demonstrate their skills, had to do so with a manual transmission. What *would* be fair is telling students at the beginning of the course that they had to learn to drive competently with both a manual and an automatic transmission.

One of the positive consequences of ensuring that students know the learning targets, the test format, and scoring criteria in advance is that it can help motivate students and help them obtain a learning goal orientation. Recent research has indicated that students are intrinsically motivated when they learn for mastery, rather than for mere performance (Ames, 1992; Dweck & Leggett, 1988). With a *learning* or *mastery* goal orientation, students are motivated by a focus on mastering a task according to established standards, developing new skills, improving competence, and gaining understanding and insight. In addition, when students assume a mastery orientation, they are more likely to see a significant link between their effort, feedback, and the outcome. This link promotes more internal attributions for success (e.g., reasons for success such as ability and effort). Finally, mastery-oriented goals lead to greater effort and involvement as well as greater interest and positive attitudes (Pintrich & Schunk, 1996).

In contrast, when students have vague information about the learning targets, the type of assessment, and scoring criteria, they tend to assume a performance goal orientation. Students are likely to focus on the consequences of the outcome, that is, a grade or some other recognition or reward, with relatively little concern about the level of understanding or learning. When only general information about the targets and assessments is provided, students find it more difficult to see the link between their effort, feedback, and the outcome.

The principle of goal orientation is nicely illustrated with gymnastics. The targets are clear and specific, and the criteria by which gymnasts are judged are public and well understood by the athletes and coaches. This results in a learning orientation that encourages intrinsic motivation. When gymnasts are judged, the assessment is usually fair because the athletes know that the same rules apply to all and they know, in advance, how their performances will be judged. Gymnasts prepare a specific routine to demonstrate their skills, knowing ahead of time that the routine is appropriate. Can you imagine gymnasts attending a meet not knowing the nature of the specific routine they should perform or how it will be judged?

Figure 4.1 shows how student knowledge of specific learning targets and the nature of the assessments used to measure the knowledge lead to more positive student motivation, engagement, attitudes, and achievement.

FAIRNESS RELATED TO OPPORTUNITY TO LEARN

Opportunity to learn is a phrase that means students have had adequate time and appropriate instruction to enable them to obtain proficiency or mastery. It

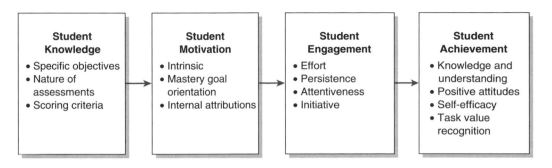

Figure 4.1   Positive Effects of Students' Knowledge About Targets and Assessments

simply is not fair if students are held accountable for knowledge and skills that have not been taught or that have not been part of the curriculum. This is especially troublesome when interpretations about the quality of schools or teaching are made on the basis of student achievement tests. Obviously, when students have not had an adequate opportunity to learn the knowledge and skills covered by the test, they are likely to get low scores. Serious decisions based on these low scores, such as school accreditation, teacher employment, and withholding of high school diplomas, are invalid due to lack of opportunity to learn. It is not so much a matter of accuracy because students indeed may not have the knowledge and skills, but the consequences are inappropriate.

At the classroom level, opportunity to learn is directly related to what teachers do and the instructional resources provided. Did students know *how* to learn the targeted knowledge and skills? Were there adequate resources for all students? Was there adequate supervision at home for homework? Did the lessons implemented cover what was on the test? Has illness or absenteeism made it difficult for some students to learn the material? How adequate was the instruction? Is it fair to hold students accountable for poor instruction? These types of questions raise issues related to opportunity to learn. Obviously, opportunity to learn is a matter of judgment and of degree, but there should at least be guidelines to identify situations that clearly limit students' opportunities so that this information can become part of the interpretation of the scores. For example, it would not make much sense to make a negative judgment about a teacher or school on the basis of student test scores based on knowledge and skills that the teacher or school simply did not include as part of instruction.

FAIRNESS RELATED TO STUDENT PREREQUISITE KNOWLEDGE AND SKILLS

It is not fair to assess students on content or skills that require prerequisite knowledge, understanding, or skills that they do not possess. Such knowledge and skills are often referred to as *enabling behaviors* because they are necessary but not sufficient for demonstrating the targeted learning. For instance, writing skills are considered enablers for being able to respond to an essay question, just as reading comprehension is needed to answer a social studies test. How can teachers avoid this potential source of unfairness?

First, it is important to identify the prerequisite knowledge and skills that are needed. For example, suppose a mathematics unit focused on reasoning skills related to fractions, and the items on the test required students to read short paragraphs to solve the problems. Successful performance on such a test depends on students' skill in adding, subtracting, multiplying, and dividing fractions *and* on students' reading skills. Students would be unable to demonstrate their reasoning if they could not read and understand the paragraphs, even if they were proficient at working with fractions.

Second, teachers need to have a good understanding of the prerequisite knowledge and skills that their students can demonstrate. Sometimes, this is done with formal pretests or other structured assessment, but more often, teachers use informal assignments and oral questioning to get a sense of whether students have the needed knowledge and skills.

A different but equally important type of prerequisite skill is concerned with test taking. *Test-taking* skills are those that allow students to maximize their performance by not being distracted by format or approach. For example, if a new question format is used, students need to become familiar with that format prior to the assessment. If students are going to be using Scantron forms for the first time, they need practice in using these forms. More general test-taking skills include the following:

- Paying careful attention to general directions and how answers are to be made
- Paying attention when reading or listening to items
- Pacing so that not too much time is spent on one item
- Being willing to skip difficult items initially and return to them later
- Answering all items if all are included in the scoring
- Learning how to guess the correct answer
- Learning how to omit wrong answers on multiple-choice tests rather than looking for the right answer
- Checking so that item and answer numbers match
- Checking answers if time permits
- Organizing essay answers before writing them
- Realizing that some items will be very difficult and not being too concerned when this occurs
- Knowing the scoring criteria for performance assessments
- Knowing acceptable formats for completing performance assessments
- Knowing how to prepare for the test
- Knowing how to handle test anxiety

Another set of skills has been identified as *test-wise* skills. These skills help the examinee identify correct answers by errors in test questions or by clues to the correct answer. Such deficiencies are common in poorly constructed multiple-choice test items. Should students be taught the following skills to maximize scores?

- Looking for grammatical clues such as inappropriate use of "a" and "an."

In a study of the effect of training on performance, the training is an

a. dependent variable

b. independent variable

c. continuous variable

d. control variable

- Looking for vague words such as "often" or "usually" that may indicate the correct answer. Absolutes are typically incorrect.

In an experiment, the independent variable is

a. measured at the end

b. always matched with a control variable

c. almost always categorical

d. the most important variable for understanding the result

- Looking for options that are longest or most precise.

If a quasi-experimental study examines the effect of training on performance, what possible extraneous variable would need to be controlled if at all possible?

a. Differences between the groups that could account for differences obtained on the dependent variable

b. The situations in which the performance is tested

c. The directions given to the subjects

d. The time of day of the training

Should students be trained in these types of skills? Although all students clearly need test-taking skills, there may be some hesitancy in teaching students to be test wise. What is important for fairness is that all students have the same degree of test-wise skills. To ensure this, it seems to me that it is desirable to inform all students about these types of skills. More generally, students should be familiar with the format and type of question and response that will be needed on an assessment. This is often accomplished by giving students practice questions or showing them examples done by students in previous years. This doesn't mean teaching the test, that is, using examples during test preparation that are identical to what will be on the test. But it does make sense to teach *to* the test in the sense of teaching students the content and skills that will be assessed.

FAIRNESS RELATED TO ABSENCE OF BIAS IN ASSESSMENT TASKS AND SCORING

A fair assessment is one in which neither the assessment tasks nor the scoring contains bias. This type of influence is perhaps the best known source of unfairness in testing. Bias can be defined as qualities of the assessment that distort performance because of the student's ethnicity, gender, race, religious background, SES, or other characteristics. Such distortion, as pointed out earlier, can distort by either raising or lowering test scores, but usually bias is associated with a negative impact (hence the phrase "biased against"). Popham (2007) has identified two forms of assessment bias: offensiveness and unfair penalization.

Offensiveness

Offensiveness occurs when the content of the assessment offends, upsets, angers, distresses, or otherwise creates negative emotions for students of particular subgroups. The negative effect influences the performance of these students, lowering their scores and reducing validity. The distressed students are distracted from what is being assessed and focus more on the offensive content. Offensiveness is particularly unfair when stereotypes of specific subgroups are present. Suppose a test question portrays women in low-status, low-paying jobs and men in professional positions. Women taking the test may be offended by the negative portrayal. The distress leads to less than optimal performance, resulting in scores that underestimate the actual knowledge of the students. Some men taking the test will also be offended by such content. Table 4.1 shows some additional examples of test items that may create offensiveness.

In large-scale testing, item writing and review procedures are used to eliminate any offensiveness in the content of the assessments. In classroom testing, however, it is more likely that such offensiveness will occur. Teachers simply do not have the time or resources to conduct systematic reviews of test content. For assessments that have important consequences, it is advisable for teachers to ask a colleague to review the content to look specifically for offensiveness, as well as other types of bias. Because teachers are often unaware that the content may be biased by unconsciously including wording or characterizations that may offend some students, a review by a colleague is helpful.

Unfair Penalization

Unfair penalization refers to bias due to the content of the assessment. This makes the assessment more difficult for some students than for others. In other

Table 4.1   Examples of Offensiveness in the Content of Assessments

Ethnicity	Juan picks beans for a living. He receives 20 cents for every bushel he picks. Juan picked 20 bushels a day for 2 weeks. How much should he be paid for his work?
Gender	The president of General Mix has held his present position for 10 years. His secretary has been with him for all 10 years. She has received a 4 percent raise each year, whereas the president has received a 10 percent raise each year. If the president started at a salary of $100,000 and his secretary at $10,000, what is the current difference in their salaries?
Race	Write a 2-page essay on the following: African American teenagers constitute 10 percent of the population, but 30 percent of the crime in this city is committed by African American teenagers. How do you explain the difference in these percentages?
Religion	Write a 200-word essay on how right-wing Republican Christians have influenced the outcome of the past two presidential elections with their extremist views.

words, bias is present when a disadvantage is given to one group or individual because of gender, SES, race, language, or other characteristic. This is the type of unfairness when the simple phrase "this is a biased test" is used. The content makes it harder for some students to score well because of factors unrelated to what they are learning in school.

Suppose you take a test that measures your aptitude by using mostly rural, farm-oriented content. The items cover such topics as types of cows and pigs, farm equipment, and winter crops. If you grew up in a city or suburb, do you think your score would be as high as the scores of students who grew up on a farm? Similarly, is it fair to compare students whose primary language is Spanish with students whose primary language is English on English oral reading skills? Do test items containing sports content give boys an unfair advantage over girls because the boys are more familiar with sports? In each case, membership in a particular group or background unrelated to instruction influences the score. Further examples of unfair penalization are illustrated in Table 4.2.

Suppose test scores are different for specific subgroups. This may or may not mean that the assessment is biased. For example, if Hispanic students score lower, overall, on the SAT, this does not mean that these tests are culturally biased and unfairly penalize Hispanic students. The actual content of the tests needs to be analyzed to determine bias. While publishing companies are careful to exclude any content that may unfairly penalize students of certain groups, it is virtually impossible to remove all types of bias from such tests. Questions need to be written with some type of content, and invariably this content will unfairly penalize some students to some degree.

In the increasingly diverse culture of the United States, student differences reflected in vocabulary, prior experience, skills, and values may influence both

Table 4.2   Examples of Unfair Penalization

Socioeconomic background	Students are required to pass a computer competency test to be promoted to high school.
Socioeconomic background	Students are required to work in small groups to plan a trip from their school to Washington, DC. In their plans, they must include expenses and an itinerary of activities. The plans will be graded on comprehensiveness and practicality.
Religion	What is the Koran?
Location	Write a persuasive essay about using hiking as recreation. In your answer, compare hiking with sailing.
Gender	Dale Earnhardt's car traveled at 180.5 miles per hour for the entire race. How many seconds did it take him to finish the 200-mile race?

formal and informal assessments. Consider the impact of the following cultural differences (McMillan, 2007a):

- Knowledge from the immediate environment of the student provides a vocabulary as well as an indication of the importance or relevance of assessment tasks (e.g., large city, ethnic neighborhood, rural, coastal, and farm).
- Depending on the culture in which the student lives, there may be different norms and rules for sharing beliefs, discussion, asking questions, taking turns, and expressing opinions.
- Respect and politeness may be expressed differently by students from different cultures (e.g., silence, squinting as a way to say no, looking up or down when asked a question, and not looking into another's eyes when answering a question).
- Learning style differences may influence a student's confidence and motivation to complete certain assessment tasks (e.g., preferences for working alone or in a group, learning by listening or reading, ability to think analytically or globally, and tendency to answer reflectively or impulsively).

The influences of these differences will be minimized to the extent that teachers and administrators first understand them, then review assessments for possible bias, and finally incorporate possible limitations because of bias in their interpretations of student performance. The differential impact of cultures is also minimized by using multiple assessments with varying formats. This helps students show their progress toward achieving the learning target and results in more valid inferences about their progress. If one assessment technique or approach advantages students from one type of background, another technique may be a disadvantage to those same students. Using different types of assessments provides a balance to the others. For example, students who perform poorly on an oral test may perform well on a written test. This points out an important principle in all assessments: *Never rely solely on one method of assessment.* This doesn't mean that you should arbitrarily select different assessment methods. Use a variety of assessments that provide the fairest indication of performance for all students.

FAIRNESS RELATED TO AVOIDING STEREOTYPES

In making judgments about students, it is only natural to form and use beliefs related to how students are likely to perform. These beliefs about what students are capable of knowing or doing are called *expectations*. Expectations are not necessarily bad. Realistic, accurate expectations are helpful in designing appropriate instruction. Expectations that are biased because of membership in a particular group, however, need to be avoided. When such expectations occur, the stereotypes will influence expectations and the nature of subjective judgments. Here are some examples of stereotypes in education:

"Jocks aren't very bright."

"Girls do better in most subjects than boys."

"Girls do poorly in mathematics."

"Kids from the south side are great athletes but are weak academically."

"A single-parent home means the father won't be involved."

In its most negative form, inappropriate use of stereotypes is self-fulfilling and detrimental. For example, if a teacher has a stereotype about students from a certain ethnic background and that stereotype is translated into behaviors toward the students, then the students may interpret that behavior as an indicator of their capability. Should students perform consistently with the communicated level of performance, the teacher or administrator will in turn interpret this as evidence to reinforce the original stereotype. A useful way to think about such stereotypes is to consider when they are made in relation to assessments, that is, prior to, during, or after instruction.

Stereotypes Prior to Instruction or Assessment

A hallmark of an effective teacher is to match instructional activities with the capabilities that students bring to school. Teachers need to assess these capabilities prior to making final decisions about instruction. Such assessment occurs before school begins, continues during the first week or two of the new school year, and occurs again during the year when beginning new units. During these "preinstructional" times, information is gathered and interpreted to answer such questions as the following:

Do students have the content knowledge and skills to handle the new material?

In what aspects of the content will students be most interested?

How can I take into account backgrounds of students to maximize motivation?

How much heterogeneity will there be in the class? How can I accommodate students who are behind others?

Stereotypes develop when interpretations and conclusions are based on fragmented or partial information. Consider the following examples:

"John comes from a single-parent family; he will have difficulty completing his homework."

"Tanya is from the low-income area of the city; she will be behind in mathematics."

"This class has mostly boys; it's going to be difficult to control."

"These Hispanic students from Mott Middle School will need remediation."

"Carol has dirty clothes; she probably didn't get a good breakfast and will probably have difficulty concentrating in class."

In each case, judgments are made on the basis of stereotypes, rather than on evidence specific to each individual or group.

To design the most effective instructional experiences, it is helpful to gather as much evidence as possible about student backgrounds and capabilities. When this is done systematically by reviewing school records, test scores, and recommendations from previous teachers, it is more likely that undesirable stereotypes will be avoided. Stereotypes are also avoided as teachers interact with and get to know each student. This interaction occurs during the first week or so and, when added to other information, can provide a complete and accurate assessment.

Stereotypes During Formative Assessment

As instructional activities are being implemented, there is a need to constantly gather "evidence" from students that is focused on how much students are paying attention and learning. This continuous monitoring provides feedback to the teacher to assess progress toward understanding the content or accomplishing the skill. Teachers typically use informal observation of students to accomplish formative assessments. This involves looking at and listening to students and then interpreting their behavior. Both verbal and nonverbal student behavior is important. The goal is to obtain an accurate picture of where students are in relation to the lesson and learning targets, and stereotypes will interfere with an accurate interpretation of these observations.

Stereotypes can influence formative assessment in a general, continuous way or can be more specific to particular situations. If teachers have a stereotype about boys being on task less than girls, in general, teachers may tend to monitor boys more closely than girls. If there is an expectation that students who live in poverty will, in general, have more difficulty learning the content, then that stereotype may affect the way the teacher interprets questions asked by these students. Asian American students are often stereotyped as high achievers. If this means that silence from these students is interpreted to mean that they understand, while silence from other students means they are bored, then the stereotype has interfered with an accurate formative assessment.

On a more specific level, teachers can form stereotypes about certain students. General opinions of individual students as "able" or "bright" or "smart," on the one hand, may contrast with opinions of other students labeled as "unable," "not very bright," or even "dumb." This stereotyping can form a "halo" for each student that may distort subsequent evaluations to be consistent with the nature of the halo. For example, a student viewed as bright may give an answer that will be interpreted on the basis of the halo as much as on the basis of the quality of the answer. It is also possible for teachers' formative assessments to be influenced by primacy effects, in which initial impressions have a distorting effect on later assessments, and by recency effects, in which interpretations are unduly influenced by the most recent observation.

Stereotypes During Summative Assessment

Stereotypes distort summative assessments most in the scoring of student responses. When constructed-response assessments are scored, teachers use their judgments of the responses to interpret student progress and learning. These judgments require subjectivity to a certain extent, and it is in this subjectivity that stereotypes can lead to unfair evaluations. Suppose a teacher is grading responses to an essay question. Will knowing the name of the student completing the response mean that some type of stereotype of this student will influence the evaluation (e.g., "She never does well on these types of assignments" or "She always does great on essays")? This is definitely possible. Is it likely that a teacher would evaluate a performance assessment more positively for some students than for others solely on the basis of characteristics unrelated to the assessment? For example, will student athletes receive lower evaluations because a teacher has a stereotype that they are more concerned about their sport than about an upcoming test? Are students who belong to the drama club stereotyped as better actors and actresses, so that when judgments are made about who will be assigned different parts in a play, this stereotype influences the judges to select the drama club students for the best roles?

These types of stereotypes can be avoided if scoring criteria are specific and explicit. The more general and vague the scoring criteria, the more opportunity there is for stereotypes to influence the judgments that are made. When grading students' constructed-responses, it is best to grade one question at a time for all students, and, if possible, grade them without knowing the names of the students. Examples or outlines of answers should be generated to act as anchors in the judgment process.

It is also helpful to review the performance of test takers of different races, gender, and ethnic background to determine if performance is related to these characteristics. If, for example, all the female examinees do well and all the male examinees do poorly, there may be something in the scoring related to gender stereotypes that is unfair. As indicated earlier, differential performance by different groups doesn't mean there is bias, but if there is bias, it will be reflected in this way. The summative assessments, then, provide data that may indicate bias or stereotypes.

FAIRNESS AS IT RELATES TO ACCOMMODATING SPECIAL NEEDS

One of the most challenging aspects of teaching is accommodating students with mild to moderate disabilities who are now routinely mainstreamed into regular classes. From the standpoint of assessment of these students, it is important for legal, ethical, and instructional reasons to adapt assessment practices so that they are fair and unbiased. Legally, teachers are responsible for gathering information, through assessment, to identify students who may become eligible for special education services. Assessments are used by teachers to provide information needed to determine if students are making satisfactory progress toward meeting learning targets specified in their Individual Education Programs (IEPs). For both of these responsibilities, the law requires that the selection and administration of assessments must not be racially or culturally discriminatory. At a minimum, the law requires the following:

1. Personnel administering tests must be trained.

2. Assessments must be in the child's native language.

3. Assessments must identify specific needs, not a single, general indication of ability or aptitude.

4. Assessment materials and administration must accurately indicate aptitude or achievement without discriminating against the child's disability.

5. No single score or procedure is sufficient as a sole criterion for determining an IEP.

6. A multidisciplinary team needs to assess the child in all areas related to the suspected disability.

These provisions mean that assessment must be planned and implemented so that the score is determined by the trait being assessed and not by the disability. That is, it would be unfair to use a test written in English to determine that a student, whose primary language is Chinese, has low ability or aptitude. It would also be unfair to conclude that a student with a fine motor disability did not demonstrate understanding as reflected in an essay question because there was insufficient time for the student to write the answer. In other words, it is illegal for the score of the trait being assessed to be influenced by the disability.

Impacts of Disabilities on Assessment

Beyond these legal requirements, teachers need to make appropriate accommodations in classroom assessments because many disabilities affect test-taking abilities. Without such accommodations, scores are unlikely to be valid or reliable. Students with disabilities have specific difficulties that are directly related to assessment. These factors are summarized in Table 4.3.

Table 4.3   Factors That Affect the Assessment of Students With Disabilities

Factor	Impact on Assessment
Poor comprehension	Understanding directions; completing assessments
Poor auditory skills	Understanding oral directions, assessment tasks, and questions; being distracted by noises
Poor visual skills	Understanding written directions, assessment tasks, and questions; decoding symbols and letters; being distracted by visual cues
Time constraints	Finishing assessments
Anxiety	Finishing assessments and being able to think clearly; demonstrating best work
Embarrassment	Finishing assessments; being reluctant to ask questions
Variability of behavior	Finishing assessments; demonstrating best work

Many students with even mild disabilities have difficulty with comprehension. This means that they may not understand directions well or remember a sequence of steps required to complete a task. This is especially troublesome for abstract tasks that require reasoning or other thinking skills. For example, a question such as "How is the Canadian government different from a socialistic form of government?" would be much more difficult than "What are the characteristics of a socialist form of government?" Auditory and visual difficulties can exacerbate limits to comprehension. If students have trouble processing verbal information quickly and accurately, or if visual and perceptual disabilities make it hard to discriminate letters and symbols, then comprehension is affected. During tests, many students with disabilities will be easily distracted by visual cues such as gestures or motions of others, which disrupt their visual focus and concentration.

Time can be a major difficulty for many students with disabilities. It simply takes these students longer to complete tests because of limitations related to how quickly they can understand and process information and record their answers. Timed or speeded tests, for example, may lead to increased levels of anxiety, especially if students are concerned that their disability will make it difficult to complete the task within given time limits.

Students with disabilities may be more sensitive to feelings of embarrassment than are other students. To avoid embarrassment, they often want to hide or disguise their disability so that they will not be singled out by peers. As a result, they may want to be treated like all other students. They may not ask questions about directions they do not understand or may hand in a test when others do, even if they have not finished. Finally, the behavior of students with disabilities may vary significantly from one setting to another or from one time to another. Consequently, teachers need to be flexible with assessments and realize that at any one time, a disability may pose extreme difficulties for the student.

Assessment Accommodations

Assessment accommodations for students with disabilities can be grouped into three categories: test directions, test construction, and test administration.

Directions

Directions can be modified in the following ways:

- Read written directions slowly, and give students ample opportunity to ask questions.
- Keep directions simple and short.
- Give examples of how to answer questions if students are not familiar with the format.
- Give separate directions for each section of the test.
- Give one direction in each sentence.
- Check students' understanding of the directions.
- Monitor the students during the assessment.

Test Construction

Tests should be constructed to include plenty of white space, a font size that is not too small, and double spacing. Different sections should be clearly differentiated, with only one type of question on each page. Each page of the test should be numbered. Other accommodations to the format of the test depend on the type of item, as illustrated in the following examples.

Short-Answer, Essay, and Completion Items. Short-answer and essay items may be difficult for students with disabilities because of the organization, reasoning, and writing skills required. Long, complicated questions should be avoided. If words such as "compare," "contrast," and "discuss" are used, they need to be clearly defined. Limit the number of questions, and allow students to outline their answers. Some students may need to give an audio-recorded, rather than a written, answer, and all students with disabilities will need sufficient time to complete their answers. Word banks can be provided on a separate sheet to aid memory. Provide plenty of space for students to record their answers.

Multiple-Choice and Binary-Choice Items. Instruct students to circle their answers, rather than writing the letter next to the item or transferring their answers to a separate sheet. Make sure that response categories are arranged vertically, not horizontally. Usually, the number of alternatives in a multiple-choice item should be limited to four, and wording such as "a and b but not d" and "either a or c" should be avoided. Any negatively stated stems or alternatives should be used sparingly. If words such as "not" are used, they should be highlighted with bold print and/or underlines.

Performance Assessments. The first accommodation with performance assessments that will need to be made is with the directions. What is expected needs to be clearly explained with examples and a reasonable time frame. Certain skills may need to be modified if the disability interferes directly with performance of the skill. Assistance needs to be provided in cases in which the disability makes it difficult for the student to perform the skill. For example, a speech impediment may affect a student's ability to give a speech or oral report. In this situation, the student may need assistance in organizing and delivering the speech or report.

Portfolios. Portfolios may be an ideal type of assessment for students with disabilities because the assignments and requirements can be individualized to show progress in whatever time frame is appropriate. Portfolios could be adapted by modifying requirements to include those that would be least affected by the disability. Reflections by both the student and teacher could be included that specifically address progress despite the presence of the disability.

Adaptations in Administration of Assessments

Many of the adaptations that need to be made in the administration of an assessment are dependent on the nature of the disability. In general, the goal is to use procedures that lessen or remove the negative impact of the disability on the trait being assessed. Some of the suggestions for adaptations are based on common sense (e.g., for students who have difficulty hearing, be sure that the directions are written; for students with a visual difficulty, make sure directions are given orally). It is best to place a "Testing: Do Not Disturb" sign on the classroom door to discourage visitors and other distractions. Some students may need to be removed from the regular classroom and taken to a separate room in which distractions are minimal. If someone can monitor the assessment, the student will have more opportunities to ask questions and be less likely to be embarrassed when asking for clarification or other assistance.

Classroom teachers who are unsure about appropriate assessment accommodations should check with the special education specialist in the school. This will help the teachers understand the nature of the disabilities and what specific accommodations are appropriate.

In Table 4.4, suggested adaptations are summarized according to different types of disabilities. For many students, however, several of these difficulties will need to be addressed (e.g., students with an auditory disability may also have comprehension, anxiety, and time constraint difficulties).

OVERALL JUDGMENTS ABOUT FAIRNESS

Unbiased and nondiscriminatory assessments are developed and implemented by teachers who first know what to look for and then match this analysis of

Table 4.4   Adaptations in Administering Assessments

Disability or Difficulty	Assessment Adaptations
Poor comprehension	• Give test directions orally and in writing. • Double-check student understanding of directions. • Allow students to audio record answers. • Remind students to check that all questions have been answered. • Read the test to the student. • Use mostly objective items.
Auditory	• Use written questions. • Read slowly, enunciate, and sound out words clearly. • Arrange for students to take the assessment in a quiet place. • Stress the importance of being quiet to all students.
Visual	• Give directions and the test orally. • Minimize visual distractions. • Keep all students at their desks after completing the assessment. • Avoid class visitors in the classroom.
Anxiety	• Allow more than sufficient time to complete the assessment. • Do not tell students to "hurry up and finish." • Give a practice assessment or practice items. • Allow students to take a retest. • Emphasize ability and effort as reasons for success. • Use many small assessments. • Allow students to reschedule assessments for another day.
Variability of behavior	• Allow retesting. • Monitor closely to determine if behavior is preventing students from doing their best work.

Source: Adapted from Wood, J. (1992). *Adapting Instruction for Mainstreamed and At-Risk Students.* Copyright © Prentice-Hall, Inc. Used with permission of Upper Saddle River, NJ: Prentice-Hall.

assessment tasks and scoring with student characteristics. The checklist in Figure 4.2 is provided to help you make a quick verification of the possible ways assessments may be unfair. As teachers and administrators, we want all students to have an equal chance to show what they know and can do, and we want the content of the assessment and the scoring to be unbiased. Even one serious unfair quality of an assessment may render the results invalid. Ask yourself this question: Would all students with the same level of knowledge, understanding, and skill, regardless of their differences or handicapping traits, demonstrate similar performance? If the answer is "yes," then the assessment is probably fair. If the answer is "no" or "I'm not sure," then there is reason to believe that the assessment is unfair.

✓ Did students know the learning targets and nature of the assessment prior to instruction?
✓ Did students have reasonable opportunity to learn what was assessed?
✓ Did students have needed prerequisite knowledge and skills?
✓ Did students have appropriate test-taking skills?
✓ Was there any offensiveness in the assessment?
✓ Was there any unfair penalization in the assessment?
✓ Were stereotypes avoided?
✓ Were accommodations made for students with disabilities?

Figure 4.2   Checklist of Considerations for Determining Fairness of Assessments

5

Assessment Methods, Items, and Techniques

A key element for successful assessment is to use high quality methods and techniques that provide the most error-free and valid scores. In addition, it is important to consider fairness, positive consequences, alignment with state and national standards, practicality, and whether the methods improve as well as document targeted student learning. So, there are multiple criteria to consider when weighing the benefits and weaknesses of different methods. In this chapter we will examine how each method can be used to meet these criteria. The first two steps when choosing a method or approach in standards-based education are to be crystal clear about (1) the nature of the learning outcome that is intended by the standard and (2) the extent of alignment of standards, tests, curriculum, and instruction.

CLEAR AND APPROPRIATE LEARNING TARGETS

The initial step in good assessment is to be sure that you know what the standards are and what more specific learning targets are needed. This requires study of the standards in relation to the depth and breadth of learning that is required. It is also important to understand the criteria used to determine successful learning.

Determining the depth of learning required in a standard requires consideration of two things—the standard itself and the assessment used to measure the standard. First, you need to establish some kind of classification for learning targets. There are many different classification schemes. These include Bloom's taxonomy (Bloom, 1956); Bloom's revised taxonomy (Anderson & Krathwohl, 2001); Marzano and Kendall's Dimensions of Learning (Marzano & Kendall, 2007); Marzano and Kendall's revision of Bloom's taxonomy: retrieval, comprehension, analysis, knowledge utilization, metacognitive system, self-system (Marzano & Kendall, 2007); and Wiggins and McTighe's six facets of understanding: interpretation, explanation, application, empathy, perspective, and self-knowledge (Wiggins & McTighe, 2005).

I find it most useful to think about the three cognitive levels of learning presented in Table 2.5—knowledge, understanding, and application. In Table 5.1, the essential characteristics of each of these three levels are summarized. This classification scheme is relatively simple and is easy to use for analysis of standards, targets, and assessments. Within each cognitive level there are several variations. Another way to visualize cognitive level is to construct a continuum from low to high, or from simple to complex. Regardless, the key to knowing the cognitive level is to recognize the verbs used in the standards. For example, here is a standard:

Students will be able to identify, in correct order, steps in the scientific method.

The key verb is "identify." This is at the knowledge cognitive level and probably is determined by recognizing, selecting, or naming the steps.
Now consider this standard:

Students will be able to explain whether a set of procedures follows the scientific methods.

This represents the next cognitive level, understanding. The key verb is "explain." It requires a more complete and flexible understanding by going beyond simply recalling the steps. Here is an example that reaches the application level:

Students will demonstrate, in writing, the correct use of the scientific method to solve a novel problem.

The key verb is "solve," which requires application of knowledge and problem-solving skills.

ASSESSMENT METHODS TOOL CHEST

Once the learning standards and targets have been identified at the right level of specificity (not too small or too large or general) and understood, it is time to determine the nature of the evidence needed to assess that standard or target. This is where the tool chest of assessment methods is helpful. By building on the selected/constructed response typology in Chapter 1, the various types of

Table 5.1   Cognitive Levels of Learning

Cognitive Level	Definition	Types	Key Verbs
Knowledge	Remembering something	Declarative Procedural Recognition Recall Facts Claims Elements Comprehension	Identifies Retrieves Knows Selects Names Defines Reproduces Classifies Recognizes
Understanding	Use of knowledge to ascribe meaning	Simple Deep Explanation Interpretation	Understands Converts Translates Discriminates Explains Interprets Infers Distinguishes Predicts Compares Justifies Illustrates
Application	Use of knowledge and understanding to reason and solve problems	Analysis Synthesis Transferability Critical thinking Problem solving Judgment Designing Constructing Testing Perspective	Analyzes Synthesizes Transfers Reasons Generalizes Contrasts Infers Creates Hypothesizes

assessments can be mapped, as shown in Table 5.2. There are six major categories of methods—selected-response (e.g., multiple-choice), short answer, essay, performance assessment (all constructed-reponse), portfolio assessment, and student self-assessment (McMillan, 2007a).

What is very important is that each method of assessment has strengths and weaknesses that determine if the evidence provided by student performance reflects on the nature of the learning target or standard. For example, generally speaking, selected-response items, like multiple-choice, do a good job of measuring knowledge of a large domain of facts, where the primary evidence is based on what the student can identify or recall. Also, though, certain kinds of multiple-choice items can assess understanding and application. However, the

Table 5.2   Assessment Methods Tool Chest

	Constructed-Response					
			Performance Assessment			
Selected-Response	Short-answer	Essays	Products	Skills	Portfolio Assessment	Student Self-Assessment
• Multiple-choice • True/-false • Binary-choice • Matching	• Sentence completion • Labeling diagrams • "Show your work" prompts • Brief narrative or written responses	• Restricted-response • Extended-response	• Paper • Project • Exhibition • Journal • Illustration • Web page • Spreadsheet • Video/audio tape	• Speech • Reading • Recital • Enactment • Athletics • Keyboarding • Demonstration	• Showcase • Documentation • Growth • Evaluation	• Self-reflection • Self-evaluation

best kind of evidence for understanding and application is typically provided by constructed-response items, where students have to show their work and explain their answers. Table 5.3 shows how well, generally, particular assessments methods measure different types of standards and targets. Higher numbers indicate better matches, with 1 = *poor* and 5 = *excellent*. High numbers indicate that the nature of the evidence to measure the target is likely to be appropriate. These numbers are derived by considering the technical strengths and practical limitations given our current standards-based emphasis in both teaching and assessment.

As you will see, higher cognitive levels are best assessed with constructed-response assessment. Selected-response is better for lower cognitive levels. Put this in the context of standards-based assessment, which is mostly multiple-choice. This makes it very easy to focus on lower cognitive skills.

Table 5.3   Matching Learning Targets and Standards With Methods of Assessment

Standard/Target	Assessment Method					
	Selected-Response	Short-Answer	Essay	Performance Assessment	Portfolio Assessment	Student Self-Assessment
Knowledge	5	4	2	3	2	1
Understanding	4	5	4	4	3	4
Application	3	4	5	5	5	2

Note: Higher number means better fit.

In the next few sections, different methods are considered in more detail, with examples of both high- and low-quality test items and prompts.

SELECTED-RESPONSE ITEMS

We will briefly consider three types of selected-response item formats—multiple-choice, binary choice, and matching. They involve student selection of answers from two or more possible answers that are provided. These formats are very efficient at measuring knowledge standards and targets, especially when there is much knowledge to measure. They can also be used for understanding and application, though the construction of items to assess "higher order" thinking is difficult.

Multiple-Choice

Multiple-choice tests are ubiquitous in schools. They are best used for summative assessment to make inferences about a domain of knowledge that must, by necessity, sample the knowledge. In other words, for many summative multiple-choice tests not all the knowledge to be learned is tested. Rather, they provide a broad sampling of knowledge. This is best illustrated by high-stakes multiple-choice accountability tests. Typically, an end of year test may use 50 or so items to measure learning that has occurred over the entire year! Frequently, quarterly benchmark multiple-choice tests are used as summative assessments. A growing trend is for teachers to use multiple-choice formats in their classroom tests to prepare students for accountability tests.

Multiple-choice items begin with a *stem*, in the form of a question or incomplete sentence, and three or more *alternatives*. The alternatives contain the correct or best answer and two or more *distractors*. Stems written as questions are usually better than incomplete sentences. Questions are easier to write, more direct, more clear, and avoid the problem of grammatically tailoring each alternative with the stem.

Table 5.4 summarizes "rules" for writing good multiple-choice items. Professional item writers are typically adept at using these rules, but don't rely solely on the credentials of someone or a company name. Even experts don't always follow the rules. With teacher-made tests, it is best to have a colleague review draft items and provide feedback. Often teachers are able to come up with one or two distractors fairly easily, but additional distractors may be giveaways to students, and increases the probability that they can guess the correct answer. If a teacher added a fifth "throwaway" distractor to each question then the probability of guessing the correct answer is still 25 percent, meaning that random guessing at the answers will result in a score of about 25 out of 100, not 20 out of 100.

One of the disadvantages of using mostly multiple-choice items to assess knowledge is that students may mostly read and reread material for recognition, rather than for recall or deeper understanding. As a result, what is learned

Table 5.4   Rules for Writing Multiple-Choice Items

Rule	Description
State the stem clearly, directly, and simply.	Write the stem so that it is self-contained and unambiguous, a sentence that is succinctly stated.
State the stem positively.	Using "not" or "except" in a stem (e.g., "Which of the following is not a type of evidence for validity?") may be confusing to students and is easily overlooked.
Keep alternatives at the same complexity, length, and grammatical structure.	Alternatives that are longer, more elaborate, more detailed, or more general tend to be correct. Stems should be longer than alternatives. Differences in grammatical structure are also clues.
Put alternatives in logical order.	Putting possible answers in order from least to greatest is better than mixing them up.
Write distractors to be either clearly wrong or plausible.	Many multiple-choice tests appropriately contain items in which the distractors have some element of truth for poorly prepared students. Selecting the most correct discriminates better.
Avoid *always*, *usually*, *some*, and *generally* in distractors.	These words are irrelevant clues to the correct answer.

tends to be superficial and fleeting. Deeper learning occurs when students are required to use thinking skills to obtain correct answers. Notice how the following items, which demonstrate adherence to the rules, measure understanding, application, and reasoning.

Sally has a weekly allowance of $2.00. She is saving her allowance to go to a movie, which costs $6.00, and to buy popcorn and a drink, which together costs $8.00. How many weeks will Sally need to save her allowance to go to the movie, and buy both the popcorn and drink?

a. 4

b. 5

c. 6

d. 7

> What is the main idea in the following paragraph?
>
> Jan bought a sailboat. It took her a day to understand all the parts of the boat and to learn how to sail. Her first sail was on a beautiful sunny day. She tried to go fast but couldn't. After several lessons she learned how to go fast in the sailboat.
>
> a. Sailing is fun
>
> b. Jan's first sail
>
> c. Going fast on a sailboat
>
> d. Sailing is difficult

> What would likely happen to the price of corn in the United States if fuel for gasoline increased from 10 to 20 percent ethanol (which is made from corn)?
>
> a. Rise
>
> b. Fall
>
> c. Stay the same
>
> d. Rise initially, then fall

A particularly effective kind of multiple-choice item is called *interpretive*. In an interpretive item, the respondent is presented with information that can take the form of a map, graph, story, table, picture, chart, or figure. Questions are then based on an understanding of what is communicated in the information provided. This type of item is great for measuring application learning targets. The most common use is with reading assessments (as demonstrated by the sailboat item). Typically a paragraph or two is the basis for answering several questions.

Matching

Matching items effectively and efficiently assess the extent to which students know related facts, associations, and relationships. Some examples include terms with definitions, dates with events, symbols with names, and persons with descriptions. The primary advantage of matching items is that a good sampling of a large amount of knowledge can be accomplished quickly. Two columns of information are used: *premises*, typically on the right, and *responses*, on the left. Students match the correct response with each of the premises. Table 5.5 presents rules for writing good matching items.

The following matching item illustrates the rules in Table 5.5. Notice the complete directions, responses on the right, and homogeneous content.

Table 5.5   Rules for Writing Matching Items

Rule	Description
Use clear directions.	Students need to know the each response may be used once, more than once, or not at all.
Use homogeneous premises and responses.	Information from different lessons should not be used in the same item.
Use 4–8 premises.	Avoid a long list of premises.
Use short, logically ordered responses.	Typically responses use one- or two-word names, dates, or other terms. Don't include definitions and descriptions. Names should be alphabetized, dates ranked in chronological order.
Use more responses than premises.	There should be 8–10 responses.
Put premises and responses on the same page.	Students should not have to look back and forth between two pages.

Directions: Match the achievements in Column A with the presidents in Column B. Write the letter of the president who had the achievement on the line next to each achievement. Each name may be used once, more than once, or not at all.

Column A **Achievements**	Column B **Presidents**
_____ Wrote the Declaration of Independence	A. John Adams
_____ Last president from Virginia	B. John Quincy Adams
_____ Third president	C. Andrew Jackson
_____ Declined to run for a third term	D. Thomas Jefferson
	E. James Madison
	F. James Monroe
	G. George Washingon

Binary-Choice Items

When students select an answer from two alternatives, they are completing a binary-choice item. This includes the popular true/false question as well as other binary choices such as right/wrong, yes/no, fact/opinion, agree/disagree, and correct/incorrect. These kinds of items are based on propositional statements about knowledge or understanding. Some simple propositional statements are as follows:

Peru is in the northern hemisphere.

Grand Rapids is the capital of Michigan.

Whales are mammals.

Reliability refers to the precision of the score.

Alaska was the last territory to become a state.

These items provide an efficient way to assess content knowledge, especially in science and history. Students can quickly answer such questions, which can provide for a better sampling of knowledge than what can be achieved with multiple-choice items. They are easy to write and objectively scored. Effective binary-choice items do not try to "trick" students or test for such subtle differences that either choice could be correct. Ideally, one of the choices is clearly correct. Of course, they are subject to guessing, especially if there are clues in the items. Rules for writing good binary choice items are summarized in Table 5.6.

CONSTRUCTED-RESPONSE ITEMS AND TASKS

With constructed-response items, students have to come up with their answer. The format is such that students aren't able to answer correctly by recognition. For tests of knowledge and understanding, students need to recall information.

Table 5.6   Rules for Writing Binary-Choice Items

Rule	Description
Each item must contain a single proposition or idea.	More than one proposition or idea in an item introduces ambiguity and error.
Avoid testing for trivial knowledge.	While it is tempting, don't pick out obscure information or facts. Keep the focus on major ideas and knowledge.
Use short sentences.	Concise items allow for more to be used, reduce ambiguity, and put less emphasis on reading comprehension.
Avoid clues to the answer.	Words such as "never," "all," "every," "always," and "absolutely" usually mean the statement is "false."
Avoid negative statements.	Statements using words like "no" or "not" are confusing to students and make it difficult to understand what the proposition means.
Avoid vague adjectives and adverbs.	Words such as "frequent," "sometimes," "occasionally," "usually," and "typically" can mean something different to each student.

This is effectively achieved with completion and short-answer items. This is the most basic way we can assess knowledge—asking the student a question and requiring an answer from memory. This is done continually by oral questioning during instruction, which is effective in providing teachers with formative assessment information. When used summatively, these items stress students' ability to recall information and to perform activities that suggest proficiency.

There are many different kinds of constructed-response assessment, as shown in Table 5.2. A good way to think about these different types is on a continuum from simple to complex, as illustrated in Figure 5.1. The more complex the requirement, the better the assessment for both learning and demonstrating application and other "higher" cognitive tasks. Simple constructed-response formats, like sentence completion, which requires a short answer, are good for testing recall knowledge. Essays are more elaborate constructed-response answers and show how well students can demonstrate understanding and reasoning. Performance assessments, such as speeches, papers, projects, and portfolios, focus on what students can do with their knowledge and understanding. The more complex the constructed-response task, the more likely it is that students will be motivated to be engaged in learning. However, scoring performance for more complex tasks is more subjective and holistic. One last point before we consider some specific constructed-response formats. When students are asked to construct their answers, teachers learn more about what the students know and what they are able to do, and often such answers allow the teacher to know where to focus instruction. In other words, they are great for formative assessment.

Completion

Like binary-choice and matching formats, completion items are easy to construct and score objectively, and provide a good sampling of knowledge. They reduce or eliminate guessing, even if they may take slightly longer to answer and score than selected-response items.

Short-Answer

These kinds of questions are pervasive in education. Short-answer means that a few words, or a sentence or two, are written as the answer. This format is good for asking students to explain an answer and to show how they solved a

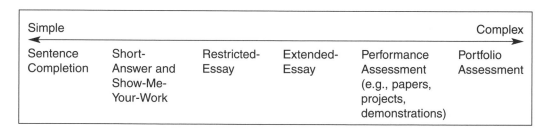

Figure 5.1   Continuum of Complexity for Constructed-Response Assessment

mathematics problem. Like completion items, short-answer is good for assessing knowledge because students must demonstrate recall and many items can be responded to in a reasonable time frame. However, scoring takes longer and there is more subjectivity involved in comparison with selected-response and completion items.

Some rules for using completion and short-answer items are shown in Table 5.7.

Essay

There are two types of essays—short or restricted-response and extended-response. In both types, the responses from students can require students to organize and integrate information, interpret ideas, give arguments and explanations, and evaluate the merit of a point of view or contention, though restricted-response essays are also used to assess knowledge and understanding. The extended-response format is best for assessing deep understanding, application, and reasoning standards and targets. It is an excellent way to show mastery of complex information, especially procedures used in critical thinking and problem solving.

One of the most important benefits in using essays is that when students know they will face an essay test, they study the material by looking for themes, patterns, relationships, and how information can be organized and sequenced. In doing so, students are learning in ways that are consistent with standards and targets that are complex and require advanced thinking and understanding. Thus, essays tend to motivate better study habits. They also provide students with some flexibility in answering the question. Finally, essay tests require less time in developing a good question.

The primary disadvantage in essays is because of the subjectivity in scoring. While there are some techniques to make grading essays less subjective, such as using a scoring rubric, outlining an acceptable answer, using a systematic system for reading the essays, clarifying the role of writing mechanics, and

Table 5.7   Rules for Writing Completion and Short-Answer Items

Rule	Description
Use questions for which there is only one brief correct answer.	Unless carefully written, some questions can legitimately be correct with more than one answer.
For completion items, place one or two blanks at the end of the sentence.	Blanks at the beginning or the middle of a sentence are more difficult for students to understand what response is called for.
Avoid verbatim language from textbooks or other instructional materials.	The goal is to measure understanding, not to encourage rote memorization of answers.
Use concise, easy to understand questions, sentences, and prompts.	Overly complex sentences and questions are unfairly difficult for less able students.

grading anonymously if possible, it also obviously takes more time to grade essays than selected-response, completion, or short-answer items.

Good essay questions are not too general. For example, these questions are definitely too general:

Explain why it is difficult for Haitian farmers.

How were World War I and World War II different?

Improved versions could look something like the following:

Describe how the weather and soil contribute to the plight of Haitian farmers. Indicate which of these contribute most to the difficulty Haitian farmers have, and give reasons for your choice.

How were the political and social factors leading up to World War I different from those leading to World War II? Focus on the five-year period leading up to each war.

The use of a scoring rubric has several positive benefits. First, it requires that the teacher think carefully about what criteria will be used in evaluating student responses. Second, it communicates to students the important elements that they need to focus on. In fact, it is best to give students the scoring rubric before they write the essay. Third, the rubric gives students more specific feedback than a single grade, though individual comments are always needed. In a *holistic* scoring guide, the teacher makes an overall judgment about the answer, giving it a single score or grade that corresponds to the levels of the rubric. In contrast, an *analytic* rubric breaks the grading into identified criteria, with a score or grade for each area. Analytic guides provide more specific feedback to students, but can impose standardization that may mitigate student creativity and individuality. An example of a holistic guide is shown in Figure 5.2, which is transformed into an analytic guide in Figure 5.3. Note how much more specific the criteria are in Figure 5.3. This format allows the teacher to score each of the five facets, then add those to reach a total score.

Rules for using essays effectively are summarized in Table 5.8.

PERFORMANCE ASSESSMENT

In a performance assessment, the teacher evaluates students' activities and/or products. There is a demonstration of a skill or competency through a presentation, report, speech, project, paper, or other process or product. The emphasis is on tasks performed by students that are created on the basis of their knowledge and understanding. This may be a presentation, such as singing, playing the

Question: In what ways were the first and second Iraq wars the same, and how were they different? Include in your answer political and geographic dimensions.

Poor	Marginal	Adequate	Very Good	Excellent
Lack of understanding of both wars; significant mistakes in similarities and differences and low understanding for both dimensions.	Partial understanding of the wars; incomplete similarities and differences and attention to both dimensions.	Mostly complete understanding of both wars; covers some similarities and differences for both dimensions.	Complete understanding of both wars; most similarities and differences correct for both dimensions.	Thorough and detailed understanding of each war; all or most similarities and differences given for both dimensions; additional insights provided.

Figure 5.2   Holistic Scoring Guide

Facet	Poor	Marginal	Adequate	Very Good	Excellent
Understanding of both wars	Does not understand at all	Demonstrates some understanding of at least one war	Demonstrates some understanding of both wars	Demonstrates almost complete understanding of both wars with no misunderstanding	Demonstrates complete understanding of both wars
Similarities	Does not address	Includes one correct similarity	Includes two correct similarities	Includes at least three correct similarities	Includes at least four correct similarities
Differences	Does not address	Includes one correct difference	Includes two correct differences	Includes at least three correct differences	Includes at least four correct differences
Geographic dimensions	Fails to include	Includes one correct geographic dimension	Includes two correct geographic dimensions	Includes at least three correct geographic similarities	Includes at least four correct geographic similarities
Political dimensions	Fails to include	Includes on correct political dimension	Includes two correct political dimensions	Includes at least three correct political dimensions	Includes at least four correct political dimensions

Figure 5.3   Analytic Scoring Guide

Table 5.8   Rules for Writing and Scoring Essays

Rule	Description
Write the question so that students clearly understand what to do.	The question should not result in students thinking "What does the teacher want in my answer?"; make the question sufficiently detailed so that it is clear what is needed in the answer.
Indicate relative emphasis in different questions.	When several essays are on one test, there needs to be an indication of how much effort should be placed on each one.
Draft an acceptable answer.	This clarifies what to look for when evaluating answers and standardizes the scoring from one student to another.
Clarify the role of writing mechanics.	Determine how much "writing" will count in the scoring, apart from content knowledge and understanding.
Score anonymously and by question, not student.	Evaluating answers without knowing the student's name, if possible, lessens the likelihood of scorer bias; bias is also lessened if each question for all students is evaluated, not all questions for each student, then on to the next student.

drums, acting, or performing gymnastics, or an original product, such as an exhibit, experiment, project, report, or paper. Often students are asked to explain, justify, or defend. Typically, the work involves engaging ideas of importance and substance; sometimes the task is authentic, something akin to what happens in actual life settings. With an emphasis on what students *do,* not with what they *know,* performance assessment is an excellent way to evaluate skills.

These characteristics make performance assessment very motivating for students, and it gives them opportunities to make decisions, solve problems, and be creative. The focus is on deep understanding and application, rather than on factual knowledge. As pointed out in Chapter 1, using performance assessment is consistent with more recent cognitive and constructivist theories of learning and motivation. While this kind of assessment became very popular over the past two decades, interest is waning in many places because of the heavy-handed influence of large-scale multiple-choice accountability testing. Often, teachers who would like to use performance assessment don't because they fear that students won't score high on the accountability tests.

Disadvantages of performance assessment focus on efficiency and scoring. Performance assessments take considerable time and result in fewer grades. This mitigates the frequency with which students are provided opportunities to show what they can do. Also, the time required for performance assessment is not entirely predictable. Despite good planning, activities often take more time than predicted. This is most likely to occur for new tasks and criteria. Scoring is typically a matter of teacher judgment according to established criteria and rubrics. The subjectivity inherent in this process can be an issue because evidence on the reliability of making such judgments is not high. It is best to have others also make some judgments as a check on both validity and reliability.

Sometimes you find that performance assessment is thought to be "authentic," like actual life outside the classroom, and some are. But some aren't as well. Authenticity can be visualized as a continuum, from unauthentic to authentic, as illustrated below.

Relatively Unauthentic	Somewhat Authentic	Authentic
← —————————————————————→		
Review diagram of a garden and identify problems.	Design a complete garden.	Design and make a complete garden.
Write a paper on zoning laws.	Write a proposal to change fictitious zoning laws.	Write a proposal for changing zoning laws that is submitted to a city council.
Explain what would be most important in teaching students to play basketball.	Show how to perform important basketball skills.	Play a basketball game.

The more unauthentic, the greater the efficiency and reliability in scoring, but the question is less relevant, engaging, and motivating. For very authentic tasks, the efficiency and reliability is lower, but relevance, engagement, and motivation is typically higher.

The initial step in conducting performance assessment is to construct the task that defines the activity in which students will be engaged. Tasks are what students are required to do, either in groups or individually. Tasks vary in complexity. Some are called *restricted-type* because there is a narrowly defined skill that requires relatively brief activity, responses, and scoring. These tend to be less authentic. Some examples of restricted-type tasks are the following:

- Construct a graph from numerical data.
- Ask for directions to _____ in Spanish.
- Sing a song.
- Recite a poem.
- Construct a poster that shows the circle of life.
- Write examples of good and poor essay questions.
- Touch type at least 40 words per minute with fewer than five mistakes.
- Use scissors to cut out rectangles and squares.

Extended-type tasks are more elaborate and complex. They take more time and are more likely to include group activities. Often several weeks will be needed to complete the activities and develop products, including time for revisions along the way. These tasks make it easier to apply several different reasoning skills to integrate different content areas. Here are some examples of extended-type tasks:

- Publish a commentary page for a newspaper.
- Create a commercial for a new product.
- Design a park from existing property in the city.
- Conduct a historical reenactment.
- Submit a bill to Congress.
- Assess the pollution in a local river.
- Diagnose and repair a leaking sewer system.
- Develop and budget and purchase products to last one week.

As you can readily imagine, these activities are engaging! Not only do students learn about the content in a way that enhances memory, persistence, and transfer to new situations, they see how schooling can be relevant to their lives. The task is rich, thought-provoking, and open to different interpretations. Usually there is no single correct answer, and often being engaged in the task stimulates curiosity and interest in other areas.

After students complete the task the teacher evaluates their performance. With student constructed responses teachers make judgments according to scoring criteria to enhance the consistency of the scoring and provide helpful feedback to students. The criteria define what the teacher looks for in the performance and/or product. The criteria are developed based on dimensions or traits that can be used to distinguish one level of competence from others. Once essential criteria are identified, a quantitative or qualitative scale is established to become the scoring rubric. Like in essays, scoring is holistic or analytical. In standards-based education one label of the rubric is something like "adequate" or "proficient" to show the minimum acceptable level of performance. Let's look at an example of these steps with analytic scoring.

1. Establish the learning target: Write a persuasive newspaper article arguing for a specific action to ease overcrowding in local schools.

2. Identify criteria:
   - Writing level is appropriate to the audience.
   - Supporting evidence is believable and relevant.
   - Sufficient detail is provided.
   - Clarity and organization of expression is illustrated.
   - Logic of arguments is sound.

3. Create a rubric:
   o An analytic scoring guide for this task could look like the following:

Inadequate	Partial Adequacy/Needs Improvement	Proficient	Advanced
Writing level completely inappropriate to the audience	Some significant aspects of the writing level inappropriate to the audience	Writing level, for the most part, appropriate	Writing level completely appropriate
No supporting evidence	Some believable and relevant evidence; some evidence not believable and/or relevant	Some believable and relevant evidence	Extensive believable and relevant evidence
Little detail	Some detail	Most of needed detail	Extensive detail
Not clear, disorganized	Generally clear and well organized with exceptions	Adequate clarity and organization	Excellent clarity and organization throughout
Illogical arguments	Some logical and some illogical arguments	Mostly logical arguments	All logical arguments

   o A holistic scoring guide for this task could look like the following:

1	2	3	4
Student writing at the wrong level with a lack of supporting evidence; little detail provided; writing unclear and disorganized	Some writing at the appropriate level with some evidence provided; some detail and both logical and illogical arguments	Writing mostly at the right level with adequate clarity and organization; some believable evidence and mostly logical arguments provided	All the writing at the appropriate level, with excellent clarity and organization; all the evidence believable and the arguments logical

○ Here is a rubric that is too general:

1	2	3	4
Superficial writing, evidence, organization, and arguments	Marginal writing, evidence, organization, and arguments	Solid writing, good evidence, organization, and arguments	Sophisticated writing with excellent evidence, organization, and arguments

Rules for creating performance tasks and scoring criteria are presented in Table 5.9.

Table 5.9   Rules for Constructing and Scoring Performance Assessments

Rule	Description
Construct the task based on context and important ideas, skills, and competencies to be evaluated.	The learning context will effect what is feasible and appropriate for the task; as in other approaches to assessment a first step is to clearly define the nature of the skills to be evaluated.
Make the task as authentic as possible.	Greater authenticity results in more student motivation, engagement, and learning.
Make the task feasible yet challenging and stimulating.	Adequate resources to complete the task are needed; students are most engaged in challenging tasks with topics and ideas they are interested in.
Develop criteria to focus on important aspects of student performance and/or products.	Not all aspects of a performance assessment, especially an extended-type, can be included in the criteria; select the most important.
Develop or show examples of work to illustrate different levels of proficiency.	Examples of products or previous student work are an excellent way to clarify the task and show how evaluative criteria are used.
Make the criteria understandable to students.	Criteria should be shared with students prior to completing the task so that they have a good understanding of what is expected.

PORTFOLIO ASSESSMENT

Portfolios consist of collections of student work—often accompanied by student self-reflections and teacher narratives—that comprise a sample of products pertaining to desired outcomes or standards. Together, the materials provide an evaluator with a thoughtful presentation and evaluation that lead to insights about the students and what has been learned. Portfolios combine characteristics of performance assessment to provide a continuous record of student progress toward meeting established standards.

One of the most important reasons to use portfolios is that they engage students in self-reflection and self-evaluation. Students think about what they know and what needs to be learned. They analyze how rubrics are used to evaluate their work. They reflect on their accomplishments, critique themselves, and think about progress over time. This provides opportunities to revise work for improvement. All of these dynamics help students to be more self-determining, resulting in a greater sense of self-efficacy and motivation. They learn as they see the link between their efforts and outcomes. "Higher" levels of cognition are used, especially application and critical thinking. Students learn that self-reflection and self-evaluation are needed to learn. There is an emphasis on self-focused learning, with less comparison to other students. Since there is typically a unique set of materials for each student, the assessment is focused on what is right and what needs improvement, rather than on how others perform, which results in greater individualization of assessment and learning. With an emphasis on continued learning, assessment is primarily formative, not summative.

Four major types of portfolios are used. The *showcase* or *celebration* portfolio includes best work as selected by the student. The *documentation* or *working* portfolio is much like a scrapbook of examples and information. The *growth* portfolio reveals change in proficiency, typically over large periods of time (e.g., several months or a school year). The *evaluation* portfolio is standardized to a certain extent with predetermined products or examples, selected by the teacher. Portfolios may also be identified more specifically, for example, as

- Literacy portfolio
- Writing portfolio
- Best-work portfolio
- Unit portfolio
- Standards portfolio
- Drawing portfolio
- American history portfolio

This illustrates the flexibility for portfolios to meet many different needs and contexts. It is an adaptable kind of assessment, one that both teachers and students can individualize.

Like all forms of assessment, there are some disadvantages. The most important are the same as those for performance assessment—scoring and efficiency. Scoring relies on subjective evaluations by both the teacher and student. Scoring criteria and rubrics are usually used to systematize the evaluation, but reliability is still an issue. Often, teachers are not trained sufficiently in procedures that would strengthen the reliability. Portfolios take considerable time, as well as resources. Teachers spend many hours to design the portfolio assignment and scoring criteria, and many more hours are spent conferencing one-on-one with students. Obviously, much time is also needed for students to create the works, self-evaluate, reflect, and provide more products. This leaves less time for more traditional teaching, teaching that more easily is targeted toward multiple, less cognitively demanding standards and targets.

The content for portfolios is varied, depending on the age level of the students, standards to be achieved, and subject. Here are some examples of different types of content:

- Abstracts of articles used for a report
- Audio and video tapes
- Essays
- Pamphlets designed by students
- Book reviews
- Drawings
- Pictures
- Letters
- Student self-reflections

Older students are able to select their own content, but guidelines and discussions with teachers are needed. Usually there are some restrictions as well as student justifications about what is included. The number of different entries in a portfolio depends in part on what type it is. One sample every week or two, to reach a total of 10–15 different entries, is typical for documentation portfolios. Showcase portfolios have fewer entries, even as low as three or four. The fewest number of products will be used in an evaluation portfolio since the emphasis is on student proficiency at the end of the instructional period.

A critical aspect of portfolios is the inclusion of student self-evaluation and self-reflection. Students need to become comfortable, confident, and accurate in analyzing their work in relation to established standards and examples. These skills need to be taught since students typically have very little time to self-reflect. Initially, simple and nonthreatening forms of self-evaluation are taught, often using teacher modeling and group projects. Students begin by taking products and labeling or characterizing them in relation to the standards and targets, as shown by scoring rubrics. Questions and sentence completion assignments can be used:

What did you learn from researching this topic?

Is this your best work?

What changed from your first draft to the second draft?

What are the strengths of the paper?

Why did you select this sample of your work?

What would you do differently next time?

This product shows that I met the science standard because _____.

The product that shows the most change is _____ because _____.

This example was selected because _____.

This paper was good because _____.

Rules for effective use of portfolios are summarized in Table 5.10.

Table 5.10   Rules for Designing and Implementing Portfolios

Rule	Description
Match learning outcomes with the strengths of portfolio assessment.	Portfolios are best for showing improvement in products that require application and other higher levels of cognition.
Allow students choice in what to include in the portfolio.	Students need to have some say in what gets included in the portfolio; this helps ensure ownership and commitment to complete the assignment.
Include the right number of work samples.	There needs to be just enough work samples or products to allow for sufficient evaluations; too many results in inefficiency.
Develop criteria to focus on important aspects of student performance and/or products.	Portfolio use criteria like they are used in performance assessment; identify the most important criteria and focus evaluation on them.
Make the criteria understandable to students.	Criteria should be shared with students prior to completing the portfolio so that they have a good understanding of what is expected.
Include student self-reflection.	Portfolios are the best vehicle for using this technique to develop positive student self-assessment skills.

Portfolio assessment was, at one time, used in some state accountability testing programs, but because of a lack of reliability and focus on limited targets this has been rarely done in more recent years. There are so many positives to using portfolios, though, that it should be seriously considered at all grade levels and subjects. Doing portfolios right requires considerable training time, for both students and teachers, yet it remains among the best types of assessment to motivate students, develop self-assessment skills, and produce higher levels of cognition.

PUTTING TOGETHER A TEST

There are a few basic procedures that will result in more accurate and fair assessments. Performance, portfolio, and essay assessments are self-contained. As long as the directions are clear and give students an indication about the time frame and scoring criteria, the procedures for developing these two types of assessment are relatively straightforward. Assessments that contain selected-response, completion, and short-answer items are often combined on the same test. This kind of test is one for which there are some additional procedures that need to be considered.

Students should know how to respond to provide the correct answer and be given plenty of time to complete the test. With experience, teachers can estimate fairly well how long students will take to answer all the items. If in doubt, make the test smaller. You don't want to create a "speeded" test in which many students do not answer all the items. Make sure that all items that use the same format are grouped together. If a test has both multiple-choice and matching items, keep all the items with each format together. Don't have a few multiple-choice, then some matching, then more multiple-choice. It's best to begin with items that can be answered most quickly.

Objective test items need to be formatted so that they are easy to read. This means that the entire question should be on the same page, that the font used not be too small, and that the print is not crowded together. A great example of how to avoid formatting problems is provided by online tests that show a single or just a couple items on the same screen. Finally, to facilitate scoring, have older students use a separate answer sheet. For younger students, put blanks next to items so that they can write in their answers.

6

Understanding and Using Numerical Data

E ven if you could avoid this chapter and its emphasis on data, numbers, and "dreaded statistics," you wouldn't want to. This is because it is essential to have a good understanding of the meaning of data and how data can be used to improve instruction. This chapter examines numerical data—scores that are obtained when student performance is measured. Here are six reasons why an understanding of numerical data is essential:

1. Numerical data can be used to efficiently summarize and describe a large number of scores.

2. Numerical data are important in determining student grades.

3. Numerical data are used in reporting standardized test scores; an accurate interpretation and the valid use of these scores depend on understanding the data.

4. Numerical data are used extensively in describing validity, reliability, norms, item statistics, and other characteristics of tests and surveys; adequate analysis and interpretation of the quality of tests and surveys depend on understanding numerical data.

5. With an increasing emphasis on school accountability, numerical data are used extensively in school report cards and other reports; teachers and administrators need to be able to understand and evaluate these data.

6. Most research uses numerical data; an understanding of the nature of data helps interpret and use research findings on topics of interest.

I will begin the discussion with the presentation of the most fundamental and important way data are summarized—looking at different types of scores.

TYPES OF SCORES

Several types of scores are commonly used in measurement. The *raw score* typically indicates the actual number of items a student has answered correctly. If 15 of 20 items are correct, then the raw score is 15. This is based on the simple frequency of items. A *frequency* is a count of items or of students. Frequency can refer to the number of students obtaining a specific score or range of scores. For example, if 10 students obtained a score of 75 and 10 students scored 78, the frequency of scores from 75 to 78 is 20.

Percentage indicates the number of items or students per hundred. Thus, if there are 25 items on a test and a student answered 20 of the items correctly, the student answered 80 percent of the items correctly. Similarly, if 15 students in a class of 30 students fail a test, 50 percent of the students in the class fail. Percentage is calculated with division and multiplication. Simply divide the number of items correct or students obtaining a specific score by the total number of items or students, and multiply by 100. For example, if 24 of 62 students obtain a passing score, it can be concluded that 39 percent of the students passed ($24/62 \times 100$). Closely related to percentage is *proportion,* which expresses the result as part of one. Thus, in the previous example, the proportion of students passing is .39.

A *percentile* score, or rank, is a measure of relative standing that indicates the percentage of scores in a distribution that are at or below a specified score. Hence, a score with a percentile rank of 70 is higher than 70 percent of the scores in the distribution. A percentile score is based on the number of items answered correctly, but it does not indicate the percentage of items answered correctly. In other words, a percentile score indicates the percentage of other scores that a student outscored. As we will see in Chapter 8, percentile scores are essential for interpreting norm-referenced tests.

Ranked (or rank-ordered) scores are those that are presented in order of magnitude (size) or frequency of scores. This indicates the relative position of each score or student. Consider the ranking of the following five scores from five students.

Score	Rank
90	1
85	2
83	3
81	4
70	5

Tied scores would yield the same rank for each score, determined by the average of the scores. Although ranking scores indicates relative position, it is a crude index of best to worst because the magnitude of the difference between the scores is not indicated. Ranked scores can under- or overestimate the degree of difference between scores. For example, if the difference between the grade point averages is small, such as a hundredth of a point separating the valedictorian and the other top four students in the class, it is reasonable to conclude that the difference between the students is, in a practical sense, meaningless. If the valedictorian scored a full three tenths higher than any other student, however, then the difference is significant. In both cases, a mere rank ordering, without consideration of the degree of difference, would have suggested that the differences between the rankings were the same.

Classroom assessments typically use raw score totals as points or percentages to grade students, give feedback, and inform parents of academic progress (more on how this is done in Chapter 8). Traditionally, standardized tests have used percentile and other derived scores. Standards-based tests may provide both kinds of scores. For example, a state accountability test may give both the number of items answered correctly and a derived score of, for example, something between 200 and 800. The raw score may be related to proficiency while the derived score is tied to percentile rank. These differences in scores can be tricky, especially when comparing scores from both or in trying to use large-scale standards-based scores to drive instruction that is then measured with classroom assessments. We'll discuss some of these derived scores in this chapter; others are presented in Chapter 7.

FREQUENCY DISTRIBUTIONS

When there are many student scores, it is difficult to understand and interpret the results as a whole without organizing the scores in a meaningful way. The *frequency distribution* is the most fundamental approach to organizing a set of data. This type of distribution simply indicates the number of students who obtained different scores. In a *simple frequency distribution,* the scores obtained are rank ordered from highest to lowest, and the number of students who obtained each score is tallied. Figure 6.1 shows how a group of scores can be represented by a simple frequency distribution. If there is a large number of scores or students, it may be best to use a *grouped frequency distribution*. In this type of distribution, score intervals are created, and the number of students whose scores are within each interval is indicated. This type of frequency distribution is also illustrated in Figure 6.1.

One disadvantage of grouped frequency distributions is that information about individual students may be lost. This problem is often encountered in summarizing a large number of scores. Although on the one hand, a single index or a few categories provide a more succinct summary, individual data are embedded within the group. To construct a group frequency distribution, determine the difference between the highest and lowest score and then divide that

Student	Score	Simple Frequency Distribution		Grouped Frequency Distribution	
		Score	f	Interval	f
Nina	98	98	1	92–98	3
Scott	94	94	2	86–91	3
Therease	94	92	1	80–85	5
Felix	88	88	1	74–79	5
Jim	86	86	2	70–73	4
Lex	86	85	1		
Jon	85	82	1		
Jan	82	80	3		
Hannah	80	79	1		
Karon	80	77	2		
Tyler	80	75	1		
Austin	79	74	1		
Tristen	77	72	2		
Megan	77	71	1		
Janine	75	70	1		
Freya	74				
Rosemary	72				
Frank	72				
Susan	71				
Benjamin	70				

Figure 6.1   Frequency Distributions of Test Scores

number by the number of intervals or categories desired. Usually, this is 5 to 10 intervals, although the actual number is determined somewhat arbitrarily. You will want to have a workable number of intervals and at the same time a sufficient number to reflect the variation in scores. In the end, you want intervals that provide the most accurate summary of the data in a condensed form. If possible, it is best to keep the size of the intervals the same.

DISTRIBUTION SHAPES

The shape of a distribution can tell you a lot about the nature of the scores. When data are presented in the form of a list, such as in Figure 6.1, it is not easy to think of the overall distribution of scores as having a particular shape. To better under-stand shape, the data can be presented on a two-dimensional graph. The scores are placed, in ascending order from lowest to highest, on the horizontal part of the graph (x-axis), and values for the frequency with which each score was obtained are placed on the vertical part of the graph (y-axis). A *frequency polygon* is created when a line is drawn to connect the frequencies of each score.

With a large number of scores, the shape becomes smoother and is often referred to as a "curve." Different types of curves provide generic information about the nature of the distribution. The most commonly used shape is the *normal curve* as shown in Figure 6.2. The normal curve represents a symmetrical, bell-shaped distribution. The normal curve is important for two reasons. First, this distribution is found in nature when most human and other kinds of traits or characteristics are measured, such as height, weight, size, temperature, wind velocity, intelligence, intensity, athletic prowess, and so on. Second, properties of the normal curve are used extensively in large-scale, standardized testing.

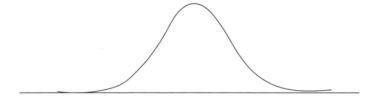

Figure 6.2   The Normal Distribution

In a normal distribution, most of the scores cluster around the middle, with few at the highest and lowest ends. Because the normal curve is symmetrical, one side is a mirror image of the other side. That is, if the normal curve is divided down the middle, the halves are the same; one is a mirror image of the other. Being bell-shaped is also important. A symmetrical curve can be shaped in various ways, only one of which is bell-shaped as apparent in Figure 6.3.

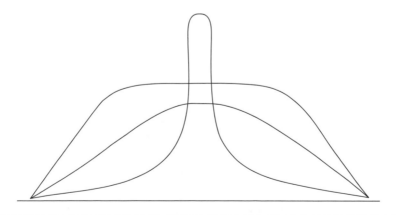

Figure 6.3   Symmetrical Distributions That Are Not Bell-Shaped

If a distribution is not symmetrical, then it may be characterized as *positively skewed, negatively skewed,* illustrated in Figure 6.4, or *flat.* In a positively skewed, or "skewed to the right" distribution, most of the scores pile up at the lower end, and there are just a few very high scores. This forms a tail that points in a positive direction. Conversely, when there are mostly high scores with just a few low scores, the distribution is negatively skewed, or "skewed to the left" (tail points in a negative direction). In a flat, or rectangular, distribution, most of the scores have about the same frequency. Negatively skewed distributions are common in classroom assessments. In these tests, often most students do well, while just a few students do poorly. (Note: Positive and negative skew does not mean good and bad!)

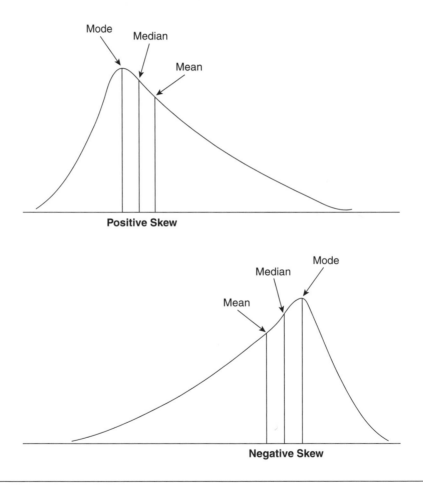

Figure 6.4   Illustration of Skewed Distributions

MEASURES OF CENTRAL TENDENCY

Although frequency distributions and curves can show how scores are distributed, there is usually a need for even more succinct indexes that can capture the essence of the distribution. These indexes are called *measures of central tendency* because they are used to indicate, with a single number, the most typical or "average" score.

Mean

The *mean* is the arithmetic average. It is calculated by adding all the scores in the distribution and then dividing that sum by the number of scores. The mean is represented by $\overline{X}$ or M. For the set of scores in Figure 6.1, the mean is 81.

One drawback of the mean as a measure of the typical score is that it may be distorted with extremely high or low scores. Consider the following distributions and means. The distributions as a whole are the same with the exceptions of two scores. Yet this small difference results in vastly different means.

1. 1, 2, 2, 3, 4, 4, 5, 5, 5, 6, 6, 8, 8, 8, 10   mean = 5.13

2. 1, 2, 2, 3, 4, 4, 5, 5, 5, 6, 6, 8, 8, 80, 100   mean = 15.93

Because the mean is pulled in a positive direction in a distribution with a few atypical high scores, the distribution is positively skewed. It is as if the mean is skewed in a positive direction. The opposite is true for a distribution with a few very low scores that tend to skew the mean in a negative direction. This is what happens to students when a zero is averaged in as one of the scores in calculating interim or semester grades. The zero may distort the mean so much that it no longer indicates the typical performance of the student.

Another use of the mean is to examine the overall performance of a class or school. Typically, a class or school average is computed and compared with other classes or schools and/or performance in earlier years. Important issues are involved when using the data in these ways. First, just as an extreme score can significantly affect the average for individual students, it also can affect the average for a class or school. This means that a few very low scores can skew the average for the entire class. Consequently, when analyzing scores for the class as a whole, it is prudent to examine the frequency distribution along with the mean. This will show extreme scores and clusters of scores that will help make interpretations more accurate.

Second, teachers find class averages most useful when the data are reported for subgroups of students and knowledge or skills. The mean score for students in a class who have demonstrated very high achievement in previous quizzes, homework, in-class worksheets, and other assignments should be higher than the mean score of students who have struggled with the content. This type of report helps validate the interpretation that high scores indeed suggest high achievement. By breaking an overall mean into subscales or parts, the teacher is able to use these results in a diagnostic way to identify areas that may need further instruction or even remediation.

Third, comparing mean scores with the scores of students from previous years, or with students from other schools, requires care because although the scores are based on the same test, there are invariably differences in other factors that affect the average score, such as ability levels of students, motivation, and administration procedures. For example, in one school, all students may take the test, whereas in another school, students whose primary language is not English are exempted. For a variety of reasons, students as a group change from year to year, so even longitudinal data from the same school can be misleading if these differences are not taken into account in interpreting the averages.

Median and Mode

The *median* is the midpoint or middle point of the distribution. In other words, the median is the value of the score that has 50 percent of the scores below it and 50 percent of the scores above it. Thus, the median is the score that is at the 50th percentile. The median is found by rank ordering every score in the distribution, including each score that is the same, and locating the score that has half of the scores above it and half below it. For the distribution in Figure 6.1, the median is 80 (in distributions that have an even number of scores, the median is the sum of the two middle scores divided by 2). The median is not distorted by extreme low or high scores and is a better indication of typical score in skewed distributions than the mean.

The *mode* is simply the score that occurs most frequently. In the distribution in Figure 6.1, more students scored an 80 (three) than any other score, so the mode is 80. In some distributions, there can be more than a single mode. For example, if two scores occur the same and both are the highest frequency scores, the distribution is *bimodal*.

In a normal distribution, the mean, median, and mode are the same. In a positively skewed distribution, the mean is greater than the median and mode, whereas in a negatively skewed distribution, the mean is less than the median and mode. The relationship between the three measures of central tendency is illustrated in skewed distributions in Figure 6.4.

MEASURES OF DISPERSION

Although a measure of central tendency is a good indicator of the most typical score in a particular group, it is also useful to know something about how much the scores cluster around the mean or median. Statistics that show how much the scores spread out from the mean are called measures of *dispersion* or measures of *variability*. If the scores are highly dispersed, different, scattered, spread, or dissimilar, then the distribution is characterized as having high *variability* or *variance*. That is, the scores vary considerably. If the scores are bunched together close to the mean, then there is little dispersion and low variability or small variance.

The need for a measure of dispersion to describe a distribution is illustrated in Figure 6.5. These two distributions have the same mean, median, and mode but portray different groups of scores. A complete description is possible only if a measure of dispersion is included.

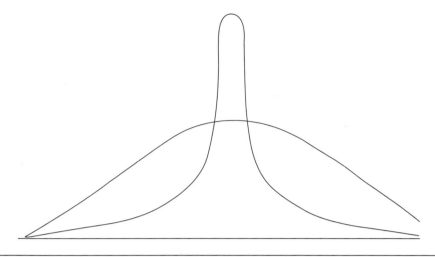

Figure 6.5   Distributions With Different Score Dispersion

Although it is sometimes helpful to use general terms such as *small, large, great, little,* and *high* to describe the amount of dispersion in the distribution, three measures are typically used to more specifically indicate variance: range, interquartile range, and standard deviation.

Range and Interquartile Range

The *range* is simply the numerical difference between the highest and lowest scores in the distribution. It is calculated by subtracting the lowest score from the highest score. The range is a crude measure of dispersion because it is based on only two scores from the distribution, and it does not indicate anything about relative cluster of scores. In a highly skewed distribution, the range is particularly misleading, suggesting a higher degree of dispersion than actually exists.

The *interquartile range* indicates the middle 50 percent of the scores in the distribution. By limiting the measure to the middle 50 percent of the scores, the majority of the scores are included in the calculation of dispersion, but extreme high or low scores that would influence the range are excluded. The interquartile range is determined by subtracting the score at the 25th percentile from the score at the 75th percentile. In the distribution in Figure 6.1, the interquartile range is 13 (87–74).

Standard Deviation

A more complicated but informative and precise measure of dispersion is *standard deviation,* a number that indicates the "average" distance of the scores from the mean. A distribution that has scores that are bunched together close to the mean will have a small standard deviation, whereas distributions with scores spread way out from the mean will have a large standard deviation.

Standard deviation is calculated with what may look like a complicated formula, but the steps are relatively easy to follow:

1. Calculate the mean of the distribution.

2. Calculate the difference each score is from the mean (see Figure 6.6).

3. Square each difference score.

4. Add the squared difference scores.

5. Divide by the total number of scores in the distribution.

6. Calculate the square root.

These six steps are illustrated in Figure 6.7 with the scores from Figure 6.1.

Essentially, standard deviation is finding how much each score differs from the mean and then finding the average difference score, or, in other words, finding the average distance of the scores from the mean. Simply calculate the squared deviation scores, find the average deviation score, and then take the square root to return to the original unit of measurement. The most common convention in reporting and using standard deviation is to indicate that one standard deviation is equal to some number (e.g., 1 $SD = 5$).

In a normal distribution, there are certain properties to standard deviation that are universal and that help in understanding the scores. The meaning of how scores are related when we say "one standard deviation" is always the same in a normal distribution, regardless of the unit of standard deviation. For instance, a score in a normal distribution that is at +1 standard deviation will be at the 84th percentile. This is true for any normal distribution. If one distribution has a mean of 40 and a standard deviation of 5, a score of 45 is at the same percentile as a score of 6.5 in a distribution that has a mean of 6 and a standard deviation of 0.5.

Because the normal curve is symmetrical, it can describe the approximate percentage of scores that are contained within given units of standard deviation. This is illustrated in Figure 6.8, where 1 $SD = 5$. On both sides of the mean (15), there is a line that designates −1 and +1 SD. The negative and positive

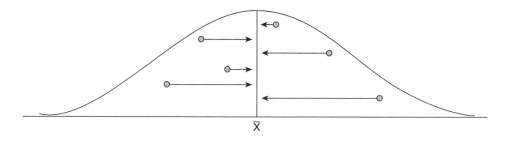

Figure 6.6   Illustration of Distance of Each Score From the Mean

Source: From James H. McMillan & Sally Schumacher. *Research in Education: A Conceptual Introduction,* 6/e. Published by Allyn and Bacon, Boston, MA. Copyright © 2006 by Pearson Education. Reprinted by permission of the publisher.

(1) Calculate the Mean	(2) Deviation Scores	(3) Deviation Scores Squared	(4) Scores Added	(5) Added Scores Divided by N	(6) Square Root
98	98–81 = 17	289	+289		
94	94–81 = 13	169	+169		
94	94–81 = 13	169	+169		
88	88–81 = 7	49	+49		
86	86–81 = 5	25	+25		
86	86–81 = 5	25	+25		
85	85–81 = 4	16	+16		
82	82–81 = 1	1	+1		
80	80–81 = –1	1	+1		
80	80–81 = –1	1	+1		
80	80–81 = –1	1	+1		
79	79–81 = –2	4	+4		
77	77–81 = –4	16	+16		
77	77–81 = –4	16	+16		
75	75–81 = –6	36	+36		
74	74–81 = –7	49	+49		
72	72–81 = –9	81	+81		
72	72–81 = –9	81	+81		
71	71–81 = –10	100	+100		
70	70–81 = –11	121	+121		
1620/20 = 81			1250	1250/20 = 62.5	$\sqrt{62.5}$ = 7.9

Figure 6.7   Steps in Calculating Standard Deviation

directions from the mean are equivalent in score units. That is, both −1 and +1 *SD* are 5 score units. Between −1 and +1 *SD* is about 68% of the total number of scores in the distribution. This is determined by knowing that if the mean is the 50th percentile, which it is for a normal distribution, and +1 *SD* is at the 84th percentile, then subtracting 50 from 84 shows that 34 percent of the scores in the distribution must be between the mean and +1 *SD*. Because the distribution is symmetrical, the same is true for the percentage of scores between the mean and −1 *SD* (34 percent). Thus, adding 34 percent and 34 percent yields a total of 68 percent of the scores of the distribution within one standard deviation of the mean.

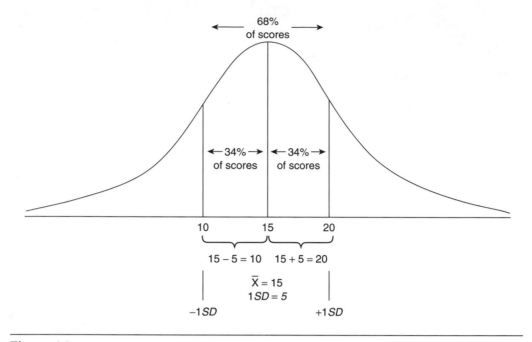

Figure 6.8

Source: Adapted from McMillan & Schumacher (2006).

Figure 6.9 shows a more complete description of the normal curve and units of standard deviation. As long as the distribution is normal, +2 *SD* will be at the 98th percentile, and −2 *SD* will be at the 2nd percentile. In other words, if a student's score is at two standard deviations above the mean, the student did better than 98 percent of the other scores in the distribution. In a normal distribution, 96 percent of the scores are between +2 and −2 *SD*.

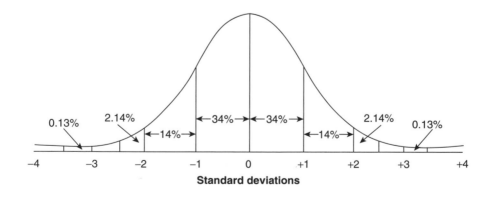

Figure 6.9   Standard Deviations in the Normal Curve

MEASURES OF RELATIONSHIP

Measures of relationship are used to indicate the degree to which two scores from different measures are related. That is, are scores from one assessment associated with, or predictable from, scores from another assessment? Suppose Ms. Lopez has a small class of students and is interested in the relationship between her classroom semester geometry test and the scores from a large-scale geometry test of the same content. Both tests are taken by her students. The scores for the students are summarized in Figure 6.10. When these scores are rank-ordered and compared it is evident that there is some degree of relationship because students who obtained a high score on the classroom assessment also obtained a high score on the large-scale test. In other words, in a rough sense, scores from one test can be used to predict approximate scores on the other test. If there was no relationship, there would be no pattern or prediction. Students with high scores on the semester test might have low large-scale test scores, and those obtaining low classroom test scores might have high standardized scores.

The kind of description of relationship shown by these two sets of scores is conceptual. Generally, a more specific and precise measure of relationship is used, known as the correlation coefficient.

Student	Semester Exam Score	Standardized Test Score	Semester Exam Rank	Standardized Test Rank
1. Molly	97	93	1	3
2. Ted	95	95	2	1
3. Dan	94	94	3	2
4. Cheryl	90	89	4	6
5. Ryann	88	91	5	4
6. Jon	86	90	6	5
7. Hannah	85	84	7	8
8. Tyron	82	85	8	7
9. Jim	79	82	9	10
10. Jan	78	79	10	12
11. Bill	77	83	11	9
12. Maria	75	77	12	13
13. Frank	72	71	13	15
14. Carl	71	80	14	11
15. Tom	68	73	15	14

Figure 6.10   Classroom Exam Scores and Standardized Test Scores

Correlation Coefficients

A correlation measures the degree to which the scores of two or more variables or factors are related. The *correlation coefficient* (*r*) is a number between –1 and +1 that is calculated to indicate the strength and direction of the relationship. A correlation coefficient is calculated by a formula and is reported as *r* = .76, *r* = –.35, *r* = .04, and so on (notice that there is a minus sign before a negative correlation but no plus sign in front of a positive correlation). Although there are a number of types of correlation coefficients, the one encountered most in assessment is called the Pearson product-moment correlation. A positive correlation means that as the value of one variable increases, so does the value of the other variable. This is also called a *direct* relationship. If the correlation coefficient is between 0 and +1, it is positive. A negative or inverse correlation is indicated by a negative coefficient and indicates that as the value of one variable increases, the value of the other variable decreases. A negative or inverse correlation is represented by a number between 0 and –1.

A positive correlation is not necessarily any better than a negative one. For example, a desirable positive correlation exists between time spent studying and achievement, whereas an undesirable positive correlation would be student anxiety and referrals to the counselor's office. Conversely, there are many helpful negative relationships, such as those between student attention and teacher rebukes, or time teachers lecture and student attitudes. An undesirable negative correlation would be student disruptions and student achievement.

The coefficient also indicates the strength or magnitude of the relationship, independent of direction. Strength refers to the degree of the relationship, that is, how powerful or helpful it is in predicting one variable from another. A high positive value (e.g., *r* = .93, *r* = .85, or *r* = .88) represents a high or strong positive relationship (+1 is a perfect relationship). The same is true for a high negative value (*r* = –.93, *r* = –.85, or *r* = –.88). Low values, those close to zero, indicate a weak or small relationship, whereas values midway between 0 and +1 or –1 indicate moderate relationships (e.g., *r* = –.45, *r* = .62). Thus, the strength of the relationship becomes stronger as the correlation coefficient approaches either +1 or –1 from 0. This is illustrated in Figure 6.11.

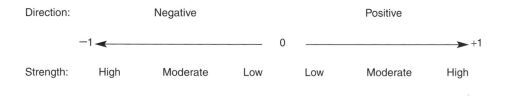

Figure 6.11   Correlation Strength and Direction

Scatterplots

Although the correlation coefficient is used extensively to report relationships, the scatterplot or scatter diagram is needed to interpret the coefficient correctly. The scatterplot is a graphic representation of the relationship. It is formed by making a visual array of the intersection of each student's score on the two variables or measures. The two-dimensional graph is made by rank ordering the values of one variable on the horizontal axis, from low to high, and rank ordering the values of the second variable on the vertical axis. For example, to correlate student achievement scores with self-concept scores, the range of results for the achievement scores could be placed on the horizontal axis and range of self-concept results on the vertical axis. This relationship is illustrated in Figure 6.12 with a few students. The student scores are summarized next to the graph in random order. The intersections of each set of scores are indicated in the graph with the letters. Together, these intersection points form a pattern that provides a general indication of the relationship. Figure 6.12 shows a positive relationship. As achievement scores increase, self-concept scores also increase.

The scatterplot is helpful in identifying two aspects of correlation that affect the interpretation of the coefficient. The first is to determine if there are any atypical scores as related to the overall pattern. In the illustration in Figure 6.12, for instance, the intersection of Helen's scores is not at all consistent with the pattern. This atypical score, or *outlier,* lowers the coefficient to give the impression of less relationship than actually exists. It is similar to the effect that an extreme score has on the mean. In this case, there is a *spurious* correlation, rather than a *skewed* distribution.

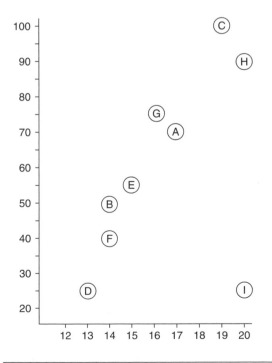

Subject	Self-Concept	Achievement
Ryann (A)	17	70
Jesse (B)	14	50
Amanda (C)	19	100
Meghan (D)	13	25
Katie (E)	15	55
Cristina (F)	14	40
Emma (G)	16	75
Jan (H)	20	90
Helen (I)	20	25

Figure 6.12   Scatterplot of Achievement Related to Self-Concept

The general pattern also indicates if the relationship is linear or curvilinear. The Pearson product-moment correlation coefficient is calculated as if the relationship is a linear one. Thus, if the scatterplot identifies a curvilinear pattern, then the coefficient will be lower than the actual relationship.

Interpreting Correlations

Because correlations are used extensively in assessment, it is important to interpret the meaning of correlation coefficients accurately. There are three primary limitations to consider: correlation and causation, restricted range, and the size of coefficients.

Correlation and Causation

It is tempting to think that a correlation describes a cause-and-effect relationship, but that is rarely the case. An accurate interpretation of a correlation *always* begins with the understanding that the relationship is descriptive only of a predictive relationship—that to some degree, the value of one variable or measure can be predicted from knowledge of value for another one. You should not conclude that one variable *caused* the change in the other or was the *reason* that the values of the other measure or variable changed.

Correlation does not imply causation for two reasons. First, a relationship between A and B may be high, but there is no way to know if A caused B or B caused A. For example, consider the relationship between achievement and self-concept illustrated in Figure 6.12. Although it is clearly positive, we don't know if achievement affects self-concept, or if self-concept influences achievement. That is, it would be incorrect to conclude that programs are needed to enhance self-concept, thinking that this would increase achievement.

Second, there may also be variables that are unaccounted for that explain the relationship. Think about the relationship between spending per pupil and achievement. If it is positive, does it mean that increased funding will increase achievement? Perhaps, but many other variables, such as those associated with family background and SES, like parental education, income, and community attitudes, are probably more responsible for achievement. Just pouring more money in the schools would not raise achievement much because of the strong effect of these family and community factors. In Figure 6.13, I have illustrated the principle of additional variables by showing a strong positive relationship between body weight and reading comprehension. Hard to believe? When you follow the steps in Figure 6.13, you see that a positive relationship is built by stringing together a series of near-zero correlations. How? A third variable, age, is related to weight, and obviously there is a positive relationship between age and reading comprehension.

Despite these two limitations, correlations are still misinterpreted to mean something causal—perhaps because it seems so reasonable, given the language that is used. For example, when there is a positive correlation between time on task and achievement, it seems obvious that increasing time on task will increase

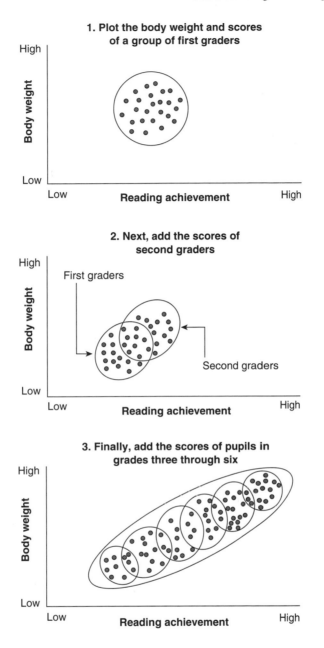

Figure 6.13   Correlation Between Weight and Reading Comprension

achievement, and in fact, this might be true. It simply sounds logical, like the positive correlation between amount of rain and growth of crops. But do not be lured into thinking that the reason or cause of increases in achievement is an increase in time on task. The reality is that we don't know if increased achievement caused students to be on task more, or if other unaccounted-for variables are actually responsible for the increases. Maybe students were given different incentives along with more study time, or maybe the increased time on task consisted of one-on-one tutoring. There are many other possible causal explanations, which if left unaccounted for, necessitate great caution in concluding that in this case, achievement increased *because* of more time on task.

Restricted Range

A second limitation in interpreting correlation is that some correlations may underestimate the true value of the relationship because the variability of one of the measures or factors is not as high as it should be or could be. That is, if the range of scores for one of the variables is confined to only a part of the total distribution, the correlation will be lowered. This is called *restriction in range*. Suppose, for example, you want to examine the relationship between grade point average and standardized test scores of gifted students. Because the range of grades and test scores of these students is restricted, the correlation would probably be small. Restriction in range is one reason why modest relationships, at best, are reported between college entrance exams, such as the SAT, and achievement in college. The range of test scores is limited to students who scored relatively high.

Size of the Correlation Coefficient

The third limitation to consider is concerned with the size of the correlation coefficient. There is a convention that a high absolute number is described as a strong relationship, but this gives only a hint of the true or actual magnitude of the relationship. This is because it is easy to think of the decimal as a percentage, so that a correlation of .70 means 70 percent of 100 percent of the possible relationship. Actually, the amount of the relationship that is common among the two variables is estimated by squaring the correlation and thinking of that as a percentage. Thus, .70 squared is .49, or 49 percent. This has a dramatic impact on what the correlation means because as the correlation lessens, the amount of relationship in common is reduced exponentially ($r = .50$, 25 percent; $r = .30$, 9 percent). This squared value (called the *coefficient of determination*) is the more accurate indicator of the magnitude of the relationship.

Another consideration related to the size of the correlations is that many will be labeled *significant* although they are small and account for a very small amount of common variance (e.g., $r = .20$, 4%). Researchers use the term *significant* in this context to mean that the correlation is *statistically* different from no relationship at all. It is probable that in studies that have a large number of participants, that a small correlation will be reported as statistically significant. This does not, however, mean that the correlation is strong, high, important, or meaningful.

The importance of the size of correlations is illustrated further in Figure 6.14, which shows scatterplots of four sets of data. The correlation of $r = .84$ shows a strong positive relationship. This makes sense for the two measures, grade point average (GPA) and SAT score. But if you look at the grade point averages that predict an SAT score of about 1000, the range of predicted scores is from 2.2 to 3.0. This is not nearly as precise as the "very strong" correlation of $r = .84$ might seem to imply. Examine the remaining three scatterplots. The one of no relationship, $r = .06$, doesn't look too different from moderate positive relationship, $r = .58$, illustrating further that the actual predictive power of a correlation is not what it may seem to be. What about the correlation of $-.17$. Can SAT score be predicted by knowing the length of hair?

USING DATA TO IMPROVE ASSESSMENTS

One of the helpful uses of descriptive data is to use summary statistics about individual items to improve assessments. With traditional selected-response tests, the first item statistic of interest is the difficulty of each item. *Difficulty* is simply the percentage of students who answered the item correctly. A difficult item may be answered by fewer than half the students, whereas an easy item may be answered correctly by all students. If the purpose of the test is to provide a norm-referenced interpretation, difficulty values around 50 percent are desirable. The difficulty index, then, informs about which items are helping to discern a difference between students in what they know and can do.

In most classroom tests, however, the interpretation is criterion- or standards-referenced. The typical difficulty index for items will usually vary between 60 percent and 100 percent. For items that are answered correctly by only a few students, review the items to determine if the scores are low because the item was poor, because instruction was inappropriate for the items, or because students in fact do not understand what is being assessed. For items that are answered correctly by all students, review the items to see if there are flaws in the items that result in correct answers even by students who do not have the knowledge and skills that are being assessed. Another way to check these items is to use them before and then after instruction in a pretest-posttest design. If students are unable to answer the item correctly prior to instruction, and then know the answer after instruction, then the item is working well to document student learning. For items answered correctly by some students, check to see if the students who answered correctly did well on other, related work and whether students who did not know the answer did poorly on related work. If both of these conditions are present, then the item is a good one.

A second procedure to use with items that are used for norm-referenced interpretations is to calculate the discriminating power of the item. The *discriminating power* of an item refers to the ability of the item to discriminate between students whose total score is high and students whose total score is low. A discrimination index for each item can be calculated by completing five steps:

1. Rank order all students on the basis of total score.

2. Divide the scores into a high and a low group (usually the top quarter or third and bottom quarter or third).

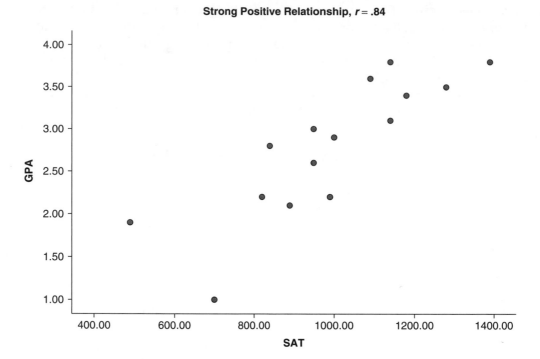

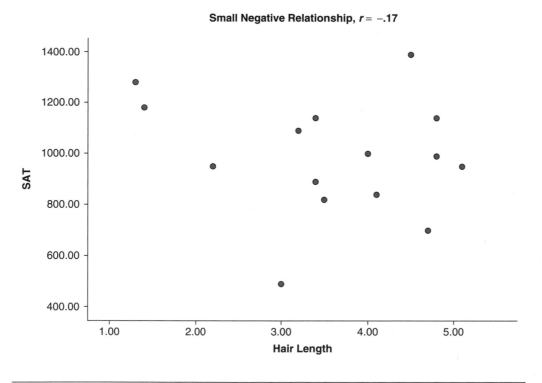

Figure 6.14   Scatterplots of Different Correlations

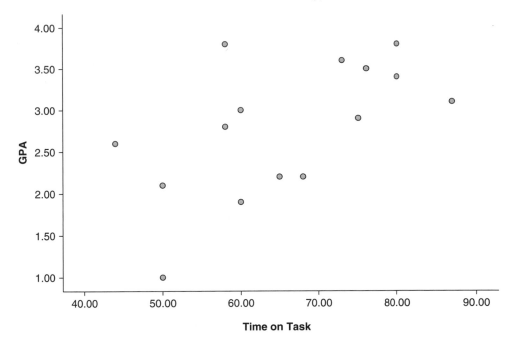

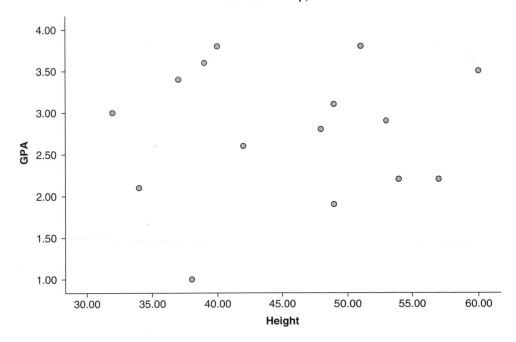

Figure 6.14 *(Continued)*

3. Tally the number of students who obtained the correct answer in each group.

4. Subtract the number of correct answers in the low group from the number of correct answers in the high group.

5. Divide the difference by the total number of student scores in the high-scoring and low-scoring groups divided by 2.

A positive discrimination index of .40 or better suggests that the item is doing a good job of separating students on the basis of what they know. Any negative discrimination index means that the item is working against the purpose of the test. Such items need to be reviewed carefully. For example, suppose a class of 20 students takes a test. Three of the top five scoring students answered question 3 correctly, while four of the bottom five students obtained the right answer. The discrimination index of this item is −.20: (3−4)/5.

Discriminating power is not as useful with criterion-referenced interpretations or with performance assessments because the range of performance is smaller, and, with performance assessments, there are few tasks (items). If the assessment is structured to provide different levels of competence, something more than simply pass/fail, then the items can be analyzed to see if they discriminate on the basis of categorizing students in one of the levels. That is, if all students categorized as "exemplary" answer an item correctly, and students designated as "fail to understand" miss the item, then the item is discriminating as needed. In a performance assessment, the same logic can be used as long as a sufficient number of tasks are evaluated. Each task is like an item.

To apply these principles, a record of the performance of nine students on three assessments is summarized in Figure 6.15. Use the principles of difficulty and discrimination to answer the following questions:

1. What is the difficulty index for each item?

2. What is the discrimination index for each item?

3. Are eye contact and voice clarity (two of many rating categories) contributing appropriately to the total rating on "Giving a Speech"?

Answers to these questions are as follows:

1. Test A, Item 1: 67%   Test A, Item 2: 33%

   Test B, Item 1: 56%   Test B, Item 2: 56%

2. Test A, Item 1: .67   Test A, Item 2: .67

   Test B, Item 1: .33   Test B, Item 2: 0

3. Eye contact: The three highest-rated students had an eye contact average score of 4.7. The three lowest-rated students had an average eye contact score of 1.7. Yes, eye contact is contributing as appropriate.

Student	Test A			Test B			Giving a Speech		
	Total Score	Item 1	2	Total Score	Item 1	2	Total Rating	Eye Contact	Voice Clarity
George	70	w	w	24	r	r	5	5	2
Ron	60	r	w	30	r	w	5	4	3
Sally	75	r	r	28	w	r	3	2	3
Tamika	83	r	w	19	w	w	4	4	1
Mica	72	w	w	24	r	r	2	1	4
Helen	88	r	r	22	r	r	2	2	3
Rosemary	85	r	w	18	w	w	4	3	5
Ashley	78	w	w	27	w	r	4	2	5
Kenya	92	r	r	29	r	w	5	5	5

Figure 6.15   Summary of Student Scores on Three Assessments

Voice clarity: The three highest-rated students had a voice clarity rating of 3.3. The three lowest-rated students had an average clarity rating of 3.3. Because the average clarity ratings of the students are the same, the voice clarity ratings are not working as appropriate.

Although data from assessment results can be used to better understand student learning, as well as to improve subsequent assessments, such analysis should always be tempered with professional judgment. Descriptive data are useful, but more as a general indicator than a precise measure that drives specific conclusions or practice. Data must be judged on validity, reliability, and fairness, along with other factors that influence interpretation or use. In other words, the descriptive data from assessments are only some of many considerations in making implications and drawing conclusions.

7

Interpreting and Using National and State Large-Scale and Standards-Based Tests

This chapter is about the use of what I refer to as "large-scale" assessments (tests), primarily to distinguish them from what is developed and used by teachers in their classrooms. For many decades educators have used standardized achievement and ability tests, which are characterized as being "large-scale" because of their wide usage. More recently, states have developed their own large-scale standards-based tests. Both of these kinds of assessments are used for many purposes:

- To identify students who may be eligible to receive special services
- To monitor student performance from year to year
- To identify students' academic strengths and weaknesses
- To identify and monitor achievement gaps
- To determine readiness for new academic work
- To select students for special programs
- To improve teaching
- To evaluate programs
- To give feedback to students and parents

- To compare schools and students
- To evaluate curriculum
- To determine if performance standards for grade promotion and graduation have been demonstrated
- To evaluate teachers
- To evaluate principals
- To evaluate and accredit schools

Some of these purposes, such as monitoring student performance through time and predicting performance, have been used to justify the administration and reporting of standardized ability (aptitude) and achievement tests for decades. In recent years, use of large-scale assessment for the last four purposes listed above has accelerated and intensified. When large-scale assessments, whether at the state, local, or national level, are used to deny students promotion in grade or graduation, to evaluate school personnel, or to accredit schools, the results of the assessments have serious implications. As previously noted, these are called "high-stakes" assessments (of course, it is not the assessments that are high stakes, but the way the results are used). Because high-stakes assessments are commonly employed at all levels, it is imperative to understand appropriate uses and limitations when interpreting the scores.

This chapter will first examine different types of large-scale tests and how they are administered and prepared for. I will also review the nature of the scores that are reported and how to interpret them. Finally, we will look at how large-scale test scores can be used to improve instruction.

TYPES OF LARGE-SCALE AND STANDARDIZED TESTS

Table 7.1 summarizes five ways of classifying large-scale tests. Each of these categories describes characteristics that influence the makeup of the assessment and the way results are reported and interpreted. With some exceptions, the categories are independent of one another. For example, a test that is national in scope could serve an achievement or aptitude function, use norm- or criterion-referenced interpretations, and be administered individually or to groups of students. The most important difference in large-scale assessments is in function.

Table 7.1   Ways of Classifying Characteristics of Large-Scale and Standardized Tests

Function	Scope	Interpretation	Level	Publisher
Achievement Ability	National State District	Norm-referenced Criterion/Standards-referenced	Individual Group	Federal government Commercial State District

Let's consider in further detail the nature of assessments that are typical in each of these two major types.

Standardized Achievement Tests: What Do Students Know?

Standardized achievement tests (standardized tests) have been a mainstay of American education for decades. The purpose of these tests is to measure how much students have learned in specific, well-defined content areas such as reading, mathematics, science, social science, and English. The tests are typically published by companies for profit, for use throughout the country. This has some important implications. Because the tests need to appeal to a broad spectrum of potential users, the material that is covered is common to most school districts. The advantage of broad coverage is that these tests measure outcomes and content that are shared by most schools in the nation. This allows significant comparisons with the achievement of other students throughout the country. A disadvantage of such broad coverage of content, however, is that there may not be a good match between the test and the local curriculum. Close inspection of the test objectives and types of items is needed to determine the extent of the match.

The most common type of national norm-referenced standardized test is the *survey battery,* which consists of a comprehensive set of subject matter tests, all normed on the same group. This type of norming allows comparisons between the subject matter areas tested to help determine students' relative strengths and weaknesses. That is, it can be determined that a student is strong in computational skills and weak in reading comprehension. It is not possible to make such determinations from different tests. Common norm-referenced standardized achievement survey batteries include the following:

- *TerraNova* California Achievement Tests
- Iowa Test of Basic Skills
- Metropolitan Achievement Test
- Stanford Achievement Test Series

In addition to providing survey batteries, publishing companies also develop tests in specific subjects, such as mathematics and reading. These tests cover a content area with greater depth and breadth. Although a subject-specific test uses the same types of items as a survey battery, there are many more questions on each subject than are found on a survey battery, which allows greater specification of strengths and weaknesses within a subject. Often, these tests are used as a follow-up to a survey battery that may have identified possible difficulties. Reading tests, for example, are used extensively to focus on a number of specific reading skills. Thus, although a survey battery may provide scores in language, reading comprehension, and vocabulary, a subject-specific reading test may examine students' decoding skills, their ability to identify the main idea in a passage, and their ability to use context to understand the meaning of words.

The primary purpose of achievement test batteries is to *survey* student learning and obtain an overall performance score for each content area as well as major categories within each content area. The results are relatively broad or general. As such, they do not typically provide teachers with much information that is helpful for instruction. To address this limitation, test publishers have developed *diagnostic batteries* for the major content areas. Diagnostic batteries, typically given in mathematics, reading, and language, provide criterion-referenced interpretations to identify a student's specific strengths and weaknesses in a particular subject. These results help teachers make instructional decisions such as whether students need remediation. For example, the Metropolitan Achievement Test series includes a norm-referenced reading survey test and a criterion-referenced reading diagnostic test. The diagnostic test provides scores in the following areas:

- Visual discrimination
- Letter recognition
- Auditory discrimination
- Sight vocabulary
- Phoneme/grapheme: consonants
- Phoneme/grapheme: vowels
- Vocabulary in context
- Word part clues
- Rate of comprehension
- Skimming and scanning
- Reading comprehension

As the nature of the list indicates, the diagnostic scores focus on areas that parallel instruction. Many testing companies offer tailor-made criterion-referenced diagnostic tests for states or districts. The state or district selects the objectives it wants measured from a large bank of objectives provided by the publisher. Items measuring the objectives are then pulled from a large bank of items provided by the publisher. For example, the Multiscore System has more than 1,500 objectives and 5,500 test items.

Some achievement batteries attempt to serve both survey and diagnostic purposes. This is accomplished by giving a score in major categories and then breaking down student performance on specific items corresponding to the diagnostic information that is useful for instruction. Because there are only a few items in each area, however, be wary of claims that the test can be both norm-referenced and criterion-referenced. In general, a minimum of 5 items is needed to make a reliable interpretation of the student's skill level or knowledge. Yet some test reports will contain 3 or 4 items for a specific area or skill, indicate how many were answered correctly, and then provide a judgment about competence. These summaries can provide an initial indication of achievement, but there needs to be further assessment to be sure about the student's strengths and weaknesses. Remember, test publishers want to sell as many tests as possible, so they do whatever they can to appeal to potential buyers who want a test that serves both norm-referenced and criterion-referenced purposes. Survey battery norm-referenced interpretations are better than survey criterion-referenced interpretations.

Standards-Based Large-Scale Tests

The most recent and very influential trend in testing is for both large and small test publishers to provide assessments that are aligned with state standards. Such tests are customized to states and school districts so that they measure state standards and, at least according to the publishers, help design more effective instruction. This has opened a very large and profitable market for test publishers who heretofore were concerned with national standardized achievement and ability tests.

In contrast to national achievement tests, however, which tend to be norm referenced, state standardized tests are usually criterion-referenced or standards-referenced, hence the name *standards-based*. The purpose of these tests is typically related to specific learning outcomes, rather than to the broader skills and knowledge tapped by national norm-referenced tests. The results of these state tests often have direct consequences for students and schools. For students, specified levels of performance may be required to graduate from high school or even to be promoted to the next grade. School accreditation may depend on students obtaining certain scores.

Most major test publishers also claim that their tests can be used for formative assessment, designed to provide information to improve achievement and evaluate instruction as well as summative achievement. Consider what Pearson, a large test publisher, says its formative assessments can do:

> Formative assessment is used to guide student instruction and learning, diagnose skill or knowledge gaps, measure progress, evaluate instruction, and report NCLB-related data . . . to determine what concepts require more teaching and what teaching techniques require modification . . . to use results to evaluate instruction strategies, curriculum and teachers, and make adjustments for better student performance. (Pearson Education, 2007)

The company goes on to show how their myriad services can meet these goals, such as alignments to state and national standards, test banks, tools to create classroom assessments, school and class comparisons, student response pads (clickers), test generators, and special reports to indicate progress over time. Teachers are able to build tests from items written by "experts." Such claims are, by and large, just that—claims. The marketing is directly addressing the need for school and student accountability. But the buyer must beware! The profit motive may be corrupting the essence of formative assessment by suggesting that the test results are applicable to individual teachers. Most importantly, these systems rarely provide instructional correctives, and often teachers don't need a constant stream of tests to know which students are struggling.

Also, such systems provide so much data that teachers and administrators are swamped with scores, buried with reports that contain student and item performance information.

National Assessment of Educational Progress (NAEP)

A fairly longstanding federal testing program, the National Assessment of Educational Progress (NAEP), has become a very important indicator of national, state, and district achievement. Since 1969, NAEP has been known as "the nation's report card" because representative sampling from the nation has been used to track student achievement in reading, writing, mathematics, science, citizenship, history, art, social studies, and additional subjects. Performance data are reported for the nation and for various subgroups categorized by region, gender, race/ethnicity, parental education, type of school, and type and size of community. Instructional practices are also surveyed and related to the achievement scores. Samples are selected carefully for each administration to allow longitudinal analyses of the results. This provides one of the few national student achievement indicators that can pinpoint progress toward increasing performance through many years. Current NAEP data are reported as scale scores (0 to 500) and according to the percentage of students placed in one of three reporting categories: basic, proficient, and advanced. These categories represent levels of achievement, and different scores are needed to be classified in one of these three.

NAEP scores are used for criterion-referenced interpretation. While NAEP is large-scale and standardized, norm-referenced data are not provided. Rather, results are presented according to the number and percentage of students achieving different levels of performance. It is critical to understand the meaning of each of these levels when using NAEP scores. There has been controversy about the labels and what they mean, especially in light of the fact that state findings may differ significantly. Recently, the discrepancy between NAEP and state results for No Child Left Behind (NCLB) has been so great that one is left wondering what is going on. Some actual comparisons of percentages of students labeled "proficient" in four states in 1997 and 2005 are presented in Table 7.2. While the "gap" has narrowed, we don't know by these numbers alone which is most accurate. In fact, many have used the NAEP scores as evidence that schools are measuring up.

The greatest value of NAEP is giving the country a standardized measure of student proficiency across years. Trends reported by NAEP are more important than the actual percentages of students reported to be in each level.

Standardized Ability Tests

Standardized ability tests measure a student's cognitive ability, potential, intelligence, reasoning, or capacity to learn. The purpose of these tests is to predict future performance or behavior. The ability that is measured is determined by both in-school and out-of-school experiences. This is how these tests differ from achievement tests. By including more out-of-school experiences, a broader

Table 7.2   1997 NAEP and State Percentages of Fourth Graders at the "Proficient" Level

State	NAEP	State Test
Wisconsin	35	88
North Carolina	30	65
Georgia	26	67
South Carolina	20	82

set of skills is measured. But the difference between standardized achievement and ability tests is one of degree. There is considerable overlap in what is covered, and often the same or similar items are used in both types.

Ability tests are developed to enable prediction of future performance by assessing current general ability (not innate capacity that cannot change). An understanding of the general ability level of students is helpful in designing appropriate instruction and grouping of students. Suppose one class, overall, has a low ability level, and another class has a high ability level. Would it make sense to use the same instructional approach and materials for both classes? Would it be reasonable to give the same homework assignments to each class?

An important aspect of standardized ability tests is the nature of the theory that is used as a basis for defining *ability*. Many theories can be used, each of which results in a unique conceptualization and interpretation. For many years, ability tests were designed to assess general cognitive ability, or intelligence. More recently, two trends have emerged. First, the language associated with these tests has changed. It is now common to call these assessments *ability* tests rather than aptitude tests (e.g., school ability, cognitive ability, or learning ability), despite little change in the nature of the initial aptitude tests. This change in language implies that *ability* communicates both innate and experiential influences, whereas *intelligence* tends to put the focus on innate, inherited characteristics.

Second, theories of abilities have changed considerably in the last three decades, stressing new capabilities and conceptualizations. Although early aptitude tests, such as the Stanford-Binet, were based on Binet's theory of intelligence, Charles Spearman's development of g (general factor) and specific factors, and Thurstone's primary mental abilities theory, later developments by Robert Sternberg (1985) and Howard Gardner (1993) have offered new insights into the nature of abilities. Gardner, for example, postulates that there are *multiple intelligences,* including musical, interpersonal, bodily/kinesthetic, linguistic, and intrapersonal. Sternberg's triarchic theory of intelligence includes the internal world of the individual (further divided into metacomponents, performance components, and knowledge-acquisition components), experiences of the individual, and external contextual abilities as three aspects of intellectual functioning. These new conceptualizations imply that although there is undoubtedly a general ability for abstract thinking, evidence for validity needs to be grounded in appropriate theory that may measure more specific capabilities that are relevant for predicting performance.

Group Ability Tests

Most ability assessments administered in schools are group tests, in which all students respond to written questions at one time. The items are usually multiple-choice to allow for efficient machine scoring. Three widely used group ability assessments are the Test of Cognitive Skills, the Otis-Lennon School Ability Test, and the Cognitive Abilities Test. The Cognitive Abilities Test for Grades K through 12 (Grades 3–12 for the Multilevel Edition) is a good example of the types of abilities that are measured. There are nine subtests in the Multi-Level Edition, grouped into three categories (verbal, nonverbal, and quantitative) that are used for reporting the results. There is also an overall, or *composite*, score, but no scores for the nine subtests.

Both the verbal and quantitative areas stress skills that are not directly taught in school, but the items require the use of skills that are learned in and outside school. The nonverbal section focuses on reasoning skills and is a good measure of reasoning abilities for language deficient students or poor readers.

Group ability tests are used primarily as screening devices. They are designed to identify students whose abilities deviate substantially from the norm. Individual assessment is typically carried out for students with suspected deficiencies.

Individual Ability Assessments

An individual ability assessment is conducted by a trained test examiner with one examinee. It is an oral test administered face-to-face. With a one-on-one administration, the results are usually more dependable and informative than are group tests. The examiner can take into consideration such variables as examinee motivation, handicapping conditions, and persistence. These tests are used routinely in the identification of educational disabilities that qualify a student to receive special education services and placement in special programs.

Four commonly used individual ability assessments are summarized in Table 7.3. The Stanford-Binet Scale and Wechsler Scales have a long tradition of use in schools. Each of these scales is focused solely on abilities. Together, the scales provide global measures of intelligence in a few major areas. The Kaufman Assessment Battery and Woodcock-Johnson III Tests of Achievement are more recently developed tests that include both ability and achievement scales. The use of results from these two assessments is similar to that of the Stanford-Binet and Wechsler scales, but because there is a measure of achievement, more direct comparisons can be made between achievement and ability. This provides a more complete picture for diagnostic purposes. As with all standardized tests, each of the individual ability tests measures different skills. This makes it difficult to compare the scores from two or more of these tests. It also means that appropriate interpretations of the results occur only if it is clear what certain scores mean. This is best understood when those making the interpretations have knowledge about the nature of the specific items used in the test.

Table 7.3 Summary of Common Individual Aptitude Assessments

Stanford-Binet Scale, Fourth Edition	*Wechsler Intelligence Scale for Children—Revised (IV)*	*Kaufman Assessment Battery for Children, Second Edition*	*Woodcock-Johnson III Tests of Achievement*
Published in 1985, the fourth edition updates the content but retains the basic structure of previous editions. Given one-on-one to individuals age 2 to 23, the test has 15 subtests grouped into four areas: quantitative reasoning, verbal reasoning, abstract/visual reasoning, and short-term memory.	Revised and restandardized in 2003, the WISC-IV is designed for use with individuals age 6 to 16 years of age. Administered one-on-one, the WISC-IV contains 10 subtests, 5 verbal and 5 performance.	Revised in 1983, the KABC provides a comprehensive assessment of both intelligence and achievement for children age 3 to 12. Sixteen subtests are combined into three regularly administered scales. Intelligence is assessed with three scales. The Kaufman is marketed as "culturally fair" ability test.	Individually administered battery of tests to assess intelligence and academic achievement of individuals age 4 through adulthood. Revised in 1989, the WJ-R contains a cognitive battery of 21 subtests (7 in the standard battery, 14 in the supplementary battery) to give a measure of intelligence, and 14 achievement subtests (9 in the standard battery, 5 in the supplementary battery).

ADMINISTERING LARGE-SCALE AND STANDARDIZED TESTS

Because most large-scale and standardized testing in schools takes place in classrooms, teachers will be responsible for administering the tests to students. It is important for the teachers to follow the directions carefully and explicitly. Instructions for the test administrators are provided in writing by the test publisher. These must be strictly followed, including any time limitations. Even if the teachers have administered similar tests in the past, the written directions should be read. The directions will indicate what to say to students, how to respond to student questions, and what to do while students are working on the test. Some portion of the instructions will probably direct the teachers to read directly from the instructions to the students, word for word as specified.

During the test, teachers may answer student questions about the directions or procedures for answering questions but should not help students in any way with an answer or what is meant by a question. Students should not be told to "hurry up" or "slow down." Teachers need to suspend their role as instructors and take on the role of test administrators. This isn't easy because most teachers want to help students do their best, especially with high-stakes tests that may reflect on the teacher. Whether the standardized assessment is national, state, or district in scope, the importance of strictly following directions cannot be overemphasized.

While observing students as they take the test, teachers may see some unusual behavior or events that could affect the students' performance, such as interruptions or students acting out. These behaviors and events should be recorded for use in any subsequent interpretation of the results.

PREPARING STUDENTS TO TAKE LARGE-SCALE AND STANDARDIZED TESTS

For students to do their best on large-scale tests, they need to have good test-taking skills for the types of items and format that are used. These skills help familiarize students with the format of the questions and give them strategies for answering the questions. As pointed out in Chapter 4, these "test-taking" skills are important because they help to ensure validity of the inferences that are drawn from the results. That is, you don't want a situation in which students have done poorly, in part, because of a lack of these skills. Here are some important test-taking skills for taking standardized and standard-based tests:

- Read or listen to directions carefully.
- Read or listen to test items carefully.
- Set a pace that will allow adequate time to complete the test.
- Bypass difficult items and come back to them later (do easy items first).
- Make informed guesses, rather than omitting items.

- Eliminate as many options as possible before guessing.
- Follow directions for marking answers carefully.
- Check to be sure that the item number in the booklet matches the item number on the answer sheet.
- Check answers if time permits.
- Review item formats and strategies to get the answer.
- Look for grammatical clues to the right answer.
- Read all answers before selecting one.

It is also best to create an appropriate climate or classroom environment for taking the test. This begins with a teacher's attitude toward the test. If the teachers convey to students that the test is a burden, unnecessary, or even an unfair imposition, students may adopt a similar attitude and may not try as hard as they can to do well. Teachers should impart an attitude of challenge and opportunity. Comments that add pressure or result in pretest jitters, such as saying what will happen if the scores are low, should be avoided. Teachers should emphasize to students that they should try to do their best and that this effort is more important than receiving a high score. Telling the students that the results are important and will be combined with other information will reduce anxiety, which could severely impair performance. If students appear overly anxious, their behavior should be noted to be included when interpreting the results. Some students may need counseling or other special services if test anxiety is serious.

Because most standardized tests use items that are fairly difficult, prepare students for this level of difficulty so that they are not easily discouraged. Give them practice items and short practice tests that simulate the difficulty of the items. Motivate students by explaining how the results will help them by improving teaching, learning, knowledge of themselves, and planning for the future.

A proper physical environment will support students' best efforts. Students need adequate work space, lighting, and ventilation. The room should be quiet, without distractions, and the test should be scheduled to avoid interruptions, such as school announcements. A sign such as "Testing—Do Not Disturb" should be placed on the door. The seating arrangement in the classroom should minimize distractions and cheating. Visual aids in the room that could help students should be removed. If possible, tests should be scheduled in the morning because students can usually focus better then than in the afternoon. Table 7.4 lists some "do's and don'ts" regarding test preparation.

INTERPRETING LARGE-SCALE AND STANDARDS-BASED TEST SCORES

On a test, students answer questions and get a certain percentage of the items correct. As pointed out in Chapter 6, this is referred to as the student's *raw score.* Although many large-scale tests report raw scores for subscales, the vast majority

Table 7.4   Teacher Do's and Don'ts When Preparing Students for Large-Scale Tests

Do	Don't
Teach to the test	Teach the test
Improve students' test-taking skills	Use the standardized test format for classroom tests
Establish a suitable environment	Describe tests as a burden
Motivate students to do their best	Tell students that important decisions will be made solely on the results of a single test
Explain why tests are given and how the results will be used	Use previous forms of the same test to prepare students
Give practice items and tests	Convey a negative attitude about the test
Tell students they probably won't know all the answers	
Tell students not to give up	
Tell students to skip and come back to hard items	
Allay student anxiety	
Have a positive attitude about the test	

Source: Adapted from McMillan, J. H. *Classroom Assessment: Principles and Practice for Effective Instruction* (2nd ed.). Boston: Allyn & Bacon. Copyright © Allyn & Bacon, Incorporated. Used with permission.

of scores that are used are modifications or transformations of the raw scores into *derived scores.* There are two types of derived scores, those that refer to the percentage correct, or *absolute derived score,* and those that are reported as a comparison with how others did on the same assessment, or *relative derived scores.* These two types of scores relate closely to criterion/standards-referenced and norm-referenced interpretations, respectively. We will begin with a discussion of norm-referenced scores—those that indicate relative position.

Norm-Referenced Scores

Percentile Scores

One type of norm-referenced derived score, percentile, was introduced in Chapter 6. As a reminder, percentile scores indicate the percentage of students in the reference group (norm group) who were outperformed. For example, a percentile score of 75 means that the student scored as well as or better than 75 percent of the students in the reference group. This gives meaning to the relative position of the score, but it does not tell much about the degree of difference between the scores. That is, the difference between scores of 80 and 85, in raw score units, is not the same as the difference between percentile scores of 50 and 55. This property makes it difficult to do much with percentiles beyond a simple description of results. For instance, because of unequal intervals, percentile scores should not be averaged.

Standard Scores

Standard scores are derived scores, transformed from raw scores, that are expressed as units of standard deviation. Each set of scores has a fixed or permanent mean and standard deviation with roughly equivalent units between the same number of scale points (e.g., a 5-point difference in performance means the same thing regardless of the location of the difference on the entire scale). This allows appropriate statistical analyses, such as averaging and comparing groups.

The simplest and most easily calculated standard score is the z score. A z score is expressed as units of standard deviation above or below the mean. The mean of the distribution is 0, and the standard deviation is 1. A z score can be calculated from any raw score as long as the mean and standard deviation of the raw score distribution is known:

$$z \text{ score} = (X - \bar{X})/SD$$

Where
X = any raw score
$\bar{X}$ = raw score distribution mean
SD = raw score distribution standard deviation

For example, the z score for a raw score of 70 in a distribution that has a mean of 80 and a standard deviation of 10 is −1: (70–80)/10. Because the z score distribution has a standard deviation of 1, these scores can easily be transformed to other standard scores that will have only positive values. These are the types of standard scores reported with standardized tests. The new mean and standard deviation unit for the converted scores are usually determined arbitrarily, which can be confusing to the public. Different companies and states will adopt unique scales. Some of these are summarized in Table 7.5.

Grade Equivalent Scores

A grade equivalent (GE) or grade norm score indicates student performance in relation to grade level and months of the school year, assuming a 10-month year. Thus, a GE of 4.6 refers to fourth grade, in the sixth month. As with other norm-referenced tests, GEs indicate a student's standing in relation to the reference group. The number is based on the performance of reference group

Table 7.5   Types of Standard Scores

Standard Score	Description
Normal Curve Equivalent (NCE)	Scores range from 1 to 99, with a mean of 50 and a standard deviation of 21.06. NCEs are similar to percentile rank at the mean (50) and ends of the distribution (1 and 99). In between, however, NCEs are not equivalent to percentile.
T-score	Distribution with a mean of 50 and a standard deviation of 10.
Stanine	Scores that correspond to nine areas of the normal curve. The mean of the distribution is 5, with a standard deviation of about 2. There is a different percentage of scores in the range identified by each stanine.
Standard Age Score (also IQ scores)	Widely used with ability tests. The distribution has a mean of 100 and a standard deviation of 15 or 16.
Developmental Standard Score (growth score)	Allows year-to-year comparison of progress with a scale that is continuous across many grade levels (e.g., mean score at second grade is 175, mean score at fourth grade is 200, and mean score at sixth grade is 225).
SAT	Distribution with a mean of 500 and a standard deviation of 100 for quantitative and verbal tests.

students on the test at different grade levels. If the reference group of students in grade 4 achieved a mean score of 32 items correct, then any student who also got 32 items correct would receive a GE of 4.6. For a GE of 4.0, students would need to correctly answer less items, say 28.

GE scores appear to be easily interpreted because of the common sense referent to grade level (year and month in school). There are important limitations to these types of scores, however. Consider Tom, a third grader who obtained a GE score in mathematics of 4.7 at the beginning of the school year. Does this mean that Tom should be promoted to fourth grade, or that he could do as well as fourth graders, or that he is performing "above" grade level? The answer is no to each question. It can be said with confidence, however, that Tom has performed about the same on the test as students in the norming group who are in the seventh month of the fourth grade. Compared with other third graders in the reference group, Tom is above average, but his score does not imply that he would be successful with fourth-grade material or should be promoted to fourth grade.

GE scores are helpful in explaining student strengths and weaknesses. For example, consider Jennifer's scores in three areas during a two-year period that includes fourth and fifth grades:

	4th Grade	5th Grade
Reading comprehension	5.6	5.8
Language	5.2	6.7
Mathematics	7.7	8.6

It is clear that, relatively speaking, Jennifer is much stronger in mathematics than in either reading comprehension or language, that there is little difference between reading comprehension and language, and that her overall performance is above average when compared with the reference group. It is also clear that she is making good progress in language and mathematics but not in reading comprehension.

Although GE scores can be helpful in identifying strengths and weaknesses, and in examining growth, a number of important cautions limit what can be concluded from the scores.

1. It is incorrect to interpret the GE as the grade level at which the student is performing. That is, a GE of 7.2 for a fifth grader does not mean that the student is performing at the seventh-grade level; it means that the student is performing the same as a typical seventh grader taking the same test.

2. Most GE scores are extrapolated beyond and interpolated between the actual data provided by students in the reference group. For example, a sixth-grade test may be given to a sample of sixth graders only during the 2nd and 10th month of the year, yet scores are calculated to correspond to every month of the school year between these times (interpolated) and also calculated to correspond to GE scores prior to and after sixth grade (extrapolated). This means that many GE scores are only estimates of student performance.

3. A unit of 1 GE should not be the standard by which progress is evaluated. This assumes uniform growth throughout a year, when in reality, students learn at different rates.

4. GE scores do not indicate at what grade level students should be placed. Grade placement depends on local objectives and the performance of all students in the school. A third grader who scores a GE of 5.0 on a test shows strong mastery of the material, but this does not mean that skipping a grade would be appropriate.

5. Because GE scores are based on the normal distribution, half the students in the reference group are expected to be above the score and half below it. Expecting all students to be above grade level may not be consistent with the achievement levels of the students or local conditions. Above-average students (in comparison with the reference group) would be

expected to achieve a GE score that places them "above" grade level, whereas a below-average class might be expected to simply reach the GE score that is consistent with their grade level.

6. Extremely high or low GE scores are problematic because of a lack of reliability for such scores and their heavy dependence on extrapolation.

7. The methods used to establish GE scores tend to exaggerate the importance of small differences in the number of items answered correctly.

8. GE scores from different tests cannot be compared because different tests of the same or similar content do not measure the same thing and because different reference groups will influence relative standing. Significant comparisons can be made only within the same test battery.

Standards-Based Test Scores

The second way scores are reported on large-scale assessments is in relation to some standard, criterion, or level of performance. With NCLB, all states have developed learning standards or objectives and assess the extent to which students demonstrate competency that meets the standards and objectives; standards-based scores and criterion-referenced interpretations are common.

The basis for interpreting standards-based scores is the number of items answered correctly or the judgment of an expert who reviews a sample of student work, such as a writing sample. The raw score or expert judgment is used to determine placement into two or more categories, such as the following:

- Pass/fail
- Meets/fails to meet
- Advanced, proficient, basic, novice
- Not proficient, proficient, advanced
- Minimal, partial, satisfactory, extended
- No attempt, inadequate, satisfactory, competent, exemplary

The score that is reported corresponds to such categories, so meaning is directly dependent on what is meant by terms such as *pass* and *proficient* and *advanced*. Accurately interpreting the scores, then, requires understanding how the standards (or benchmarks) were set and what is meant by each level. Let's consider the most basic type of standard-based score—pass or fail. Suppose a school district has identified a set of fifth-grade mathematics competencies that must be demonstrated for students to obtain a passing score on the end-of-year fifth-grade mathematics test. Once the competencies have been identified, test items would need to be generated to measure the competencies. Suppose 20 questions are developed to measure each competency. How many of the 20 items would a student need to answer correctly to be judged competent? Seventy-five percent? Fifteen correct of 20? Half the items? Twelve items? Seventeen items? All 20 items?

The determination of the standard involves making a judgment about the number of items that need to be answered correctly to classify the score as "pass." Who makes the judgment? Typically, such judgments are made by experts in the content area, though final determination of "cut scores" for state tests is made by state boards of education.

Experts and policy makers review the items and make decisions about whether students with competence in the area assessed would be able to answer the items. Of course, there is some variation in the judgments of different individuals, so usually there is some type of averaging of the judgments of many individuals. Table 7.6 illustrates how many items must be answered correctly to reach proficient and advanced levels in the Virginia assessment program for several subjects in Grades 3 and 8.

A common approach to standards-based scores is to use a scale to report different levels of competency. These scales are arbitrary and often are unique to a given test or state assessment program. In Virginia, for instance, scores on statewide competency tests, which are standards based, are reported using a scale of 0 to 600, with a score of 400 indicating proficient. The score indicating proficient stays the same for all content areas, although the number of items answered correctly is different.

Standards-based scores, then, depend not only on how well students do but also on the nature of the judgments made by those setting the standards. Accurate interpretations can be made only after inspecting the items and descriptions of what words such as *proficient* and *advanced* mean and by knowing about the individuals who set the standards.

To promote accurate interpretations, large-scale test developers release sample items and examples of student work that have been judged. These items can be reviewed to give some idea of the level of performance needed.

Table 7.6   Cut Scores Established in 2006 for the Virginia Assessment Program

Test	Pass/Proficient	Pass/Advanced
Grade 3		
English: Reading	23 out of 35 items	31 out of 35 items
Mathematics	35 out of 50 items	45 out of 50 items
Grade 4		
English: Reading	23 out of 35 items	31 out of 35 items
Mathematics	35 out of 50 items	43 out of 50 items
Grade 8		
English: Reading	28 out of 45 items	40 out of 45 items
Mathematics	32 out of 50 items	42 out of 50 items

Source: Virginia Department of Education (2007).

The more removed the test is from a local setting, the more likely it is that those setting the standards will bring perspectives and values to that process that are inconsistent with local perspectives and values. National-level tests, such as the NAEP, are further from the classroom than a state test, and a state test is further from the classroom than a district test. Thus, those setting the standards on a national or state test are much less informed about local curriculum and values than those in the district who set standards only for schools and students in that district.

Difficulty of items is an important factor in standard setting, which is why sound inferences depend on knowledge of the items. There can be great variability in the difficulty of items that measure the same competency, objective, or standard. Given this variability, just knowing that a student answered 70 percent of the items correct is insufficient. You also need to know if these were hard or easy items. Obviously, getting 70 percent correct with easy items means something different from 70 percent with difficult items. One approach to judging the nature of the standard is to compare scores from the assessment with other performances of the students. This is essentially a check on the validity of the inferences drawn from the scores. It can provide a type of anchor for interpretation. For instance, suppose your brightest and highest-performing students don't "pass" the test. These are students who have demonstrated strong achievement in similar areas in class, yet they fail to show adequate performance. Because there is good evidence that they know the skills, it may be best to explore student motivation to do well on the test and to examine the test specifications and items in greater detail to determine a reasonable explanation for the discrepancy. It may be that what you thought was adequate knowledge and skill was not, or that the test is assessing areas you did not emphasize with your students.

As previously mentioned, many norm-referenced standardized tests purport to provide criterion-referenced information. Be wary of using norm-referenced tests in this way. It is best to use norm-referenced tests for what they are designed to do—show comparisons with other students, identify strengths and weaknesses, and show growth. To make sound decisions about whether students have obtained specific knowledge and skills, criterion-referenced assessments, which are designed for that purpose, are best.

One additional and important limitation to some standardized assessments, both norm- and criterion/standards-referenced, is the common use of a multiple-choice item format that allows machine scoring of student responses. This format, along with the need to be broad in coverage, results in the measurement of mostly low-level skills and knowledge (Marzano & Kendall, 1996). Such tests tend to assess isolated facts and only rudimentary understanding. Students select, rather than produce, a response on these types of tests. The multiple-choice format also gives the false impression that there is a right and wrong answer for all questions.

One of the dilemmas of standards-based large-scale assessment is that if items are constructed to require application, analysis, synthesis, and other reasoning skills, the tests measure general ability in addition to knowledge and understanding of the content area. In Virginia, for example, the scores on the Grade 8 English tests are strongly correlated to scores on both science and mathematics. Although incorporating reasoning skills with content may be desirable from one perspective, it complicates interpretation of the results from these assessments. If a student obtains a low score on a mathematics test that correlates strongly with performance in English, is the correct conclusion that the student is weak in mathematics or weak in applying math skills to these types of tests that require competence in reading comprehension to understand the question? Do low scores mean more work is needed in mathematics, in doing the types of items that are on the test, or in reading comprehension? As I have already stressed, the scores from these tests make most sense when interpreted in light of other indicators of student performance.

INTERPRETING LARGE-SCALE AND STANDARDIZED TEST REPORTS

Standardized Achievement Tests

Many types of reports can be produced from standardized achievement tests, including reports for parents, individual students, classes, schools, and school districts. Because the reports are designed to provide as much information as possible on a single page, they may appear complicated and difficult to understand. There is typically a large number of different scores, and often graphs are provided. For a comprehensive battery of tests, scores are usually reported for each skill as well as each subskill. A good approach to understanding the reports is to first consult the test manual and/or interpretation guide to find examples of explanations of actual scores. The manual or interpretation guide is also important for understanding the meanings of the labels used for the skills (e.g., math computation, measurement, and language). Most publishers of large-scale standardized assessments do a good job of explaining what each part of the report means.

Each test publisher has a unique format for reporting results and usually has unique types of scores. Different formats are used to summarize the scores. A single report may include a listing of all students in a class, the class as a whole, a skills analysis for the class or individual students, individual profiles, growth charts, and other formats. Some reports will include scores for only major content areas, whereas others will include subscale scores or even results for individual items. Also, different types of norms may be used. All this means that each report contains different information, organized and presented in unique formats. So the first step in understanding a report is to identify the nature of the information presented, then find an explanation for it in an interpretive guide.

Two examples of state-level standards-based reports are shown in Figures 7.1 and 7.2. The Virginia Student Performance Report shows scaled scores that are unique to these tests and a proficiency level summary for each of five major content areas. The reporting category scaled scores are also reported, ranging for Elizabeth Tomlinson (fictitious) from 31 to 44. The reporting category scores are not tied to proficiency levels and provide only a general idea of student strengths and weaknesses and a general indication of performance compared with other students statewide (35 is the state average). The reporting category scores do not add up to the total test score.

The Virginia School Summary Report (Figure 7.2) summarizes the number and percentage of students obtaining each of the four ratings in three writing domains. The mean scale scores for the test and reporting categories are indicated, as well as the number and percentage of students in the school who are categorized as fail/does not meet, pass/proficient, or pass/advanced. For this testing period, 38 percent of the students obtained a passing score. The written expression and usage mechanics scores show that these areas contribute in approximate equal amounts to the total score (62 percent show consistent or reasonable control for written expression; 65 percent show consistent or reasonable control in usage mechanics).

USING LARGE-SCALE AND STANDARDIZED TEST RESULTS TO IMPROVE INSTRUCTION

The results of large-scale testing can be used for planning prior to instruction and as a way to evaluate the effectiveness of instruction after content and skills have been taught. Any use of standardized scores should be done with the understanding that the results provide only one of many sources of information. Large-scale test results should always be interpreted in the context of other evidence provided by classroom assessments and teacher observation. It is also important to understand the specific nature of the content or skills that are assessed.

Prior to instruction, results from standardized tests may provide a good indication of the general ability level of the students in the class. This information can be used to help establish reasonable, realistic expectations for students and to influence the nature of instructional materials. Expectations should not be fatalistically low or unreasonably high. If the results from a reading readiness test indicate that the class is lacking in ability to read, then they should not be the sole or even major determinant of instructional practices.

The scores in various subtests can be compared to identify strengths and weaknesses, which can help determine the amount of instruction to give in different areas. Students whose achievement is much lower than what might be expected on the basis of ability testing may need further testing, special attention, or counseling. What constitutes "much lower"? Generally, a discrepancy of 10 percentile points may be sufficient. If the percentile "bands" for achievement, which show the probable range of actual student knowledge or skill, do not overlap with the ability bands, then a significant discrepancy is identified.

Norm-referenced standardized tests are useful for selection and placement into special programs. This occurs at both ends of the achievement/aptitude distribution. Students are selected to receive special services in part on the basis

Virginia
Standards of Learning Assessments
STUDENT PERFORMANCE REPORT
GRADE 5 TESTS

Student ID#s are optional.

STUDENT NAME: ELIZABETH TOMLINSON
DOB: 10/24/85
GENDER: FEMALE
ID#   043156327690
ETHNICITY: WHITE
CLASS: M. SMITH
SCHOOL: LAKESIDE ELEMENTARY - 5678   GRADE: 05
DIVISION: NEWTOWN - 123   TEST DATE: SPRING 1998

TEST REPORTING CATEGORIES	# of ITEMS BLANK& MULTIPLE MARKED	SCALED SCORE	PROFICIENCY LEVEL SUMMARY
English: Reading/Literature and Research	0	433	PASS/PROFICIENT
Use word analysis strategies.	0	31	
Understand a variety of printed materials/resource materials.	0	35	
Understand elements of literature.	0	39	
Mathematics	0	406	PASS/PROFICIENT
Number and Number Sense	0	37	
Computation and Estimation	0	37	
Measurement and Geometry	0	39	
Probability and Statistics	0	33	
Patterns, Functions, and Algebra	0	35	
History and Social Science	0	361	
History	0	33	
Geography	0	33	
Economics	0	33	
Civics	0	33	
Science	0	400	
Scientific Investigation	0	32	
Force, Motion, Energy, and Matter	0	43	
Life Processes and Living Systems	0	34	
Earth/Space Systems and Cycles	0	30	
Computer/ Technology	0	484	
Basic Understanding of Computer Technology	0	43	
Basic Operational Skills	0	39	
Using Technology to Solve Problems	0	44	

Notes:

This *Student Performance Report* (SPR) displays scores for a student on all tests and their reporting categories except for *English: Writing,* which is reported on a separate SPR. The SPR shows, for each SOL test, the

• number of items to which the student did not respond (BLANK) and those where the student marked more than one answer (MULTIPLE-MARKED),
• scaled scores earned by the student on each test as a whole and its reporting categories, and
• proficiency level attained by the student (Pass/Advanced, Pass/Proficient, Fail/Does Not Meet).

Figure 7.1   Example of State Standards-Based Test Individual Report

Source: Virginia Department of Education (2007).

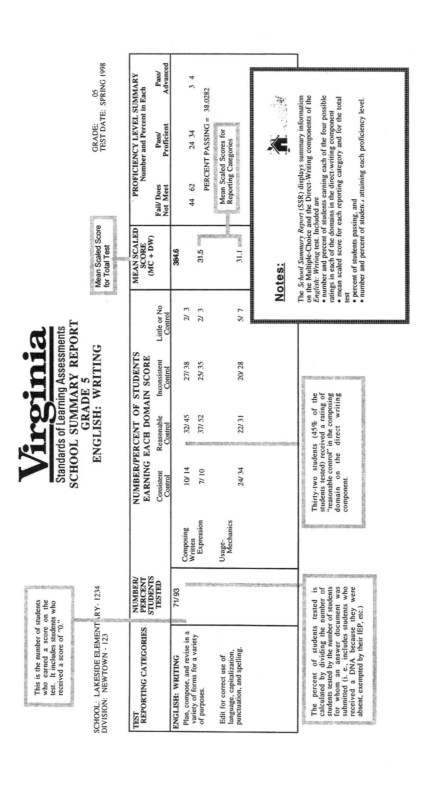

Figure 7.2 Example of State Standards-Based Test School Report

Source: Virginia Department of Education (2007).

of standardized test results; other students are placed in "gifted" programs or other advanced programs because they are identified as the brightest or most knowledgeable.

Large-scale tests given at the end of instruction, like external accountability tests for NCLB, can be used to evaluate the effectiveness of instruction and curriculum. It is expected that students should score well in areas that have been stressed in the instructional program. If not, the scores act like a temperature gauge, indicating that further information needs to be gathered, such as other test performance data and a review of the match between specific test items and subscales and what was taught. When large-scale test data can be gathered through several years, it is possible to evaluate programs by examining trends in areas that have been emphasized and in areas that have not been the focus of instruction.

When students are tested each year, the scores can be used to indicate areas within the curriculum that need further attention. If an area shows a consistent pattern of low scores despite the area being stressed in the classroom, the specific methods of teaching may need to be examined.

Perhaps the most serious misuse of large-scale tests is to evaluate teachers. This is a misuse of the results for several reasons: (a) Standardized tests are not designed to evaluate teaching or teachers; (b) the content and skills tested will not have a perfect match with local curriculum or what individual teachers stress in the classroom; (c) each year brings a unique group of students to a teacher, with knowledge, skills, motivation, and group chemistry that may be different from other years; (d) it is difficult, if not impossible, to isolate the influence of differences between teachers (most of what students experience is common); and (e) a large-scale test provides only one indication of student performance.

In summary, most teachers will find large-scale test results helpful *as long as the scores are used with a full understanding of their limitations and as a supplement to data gathered directly from students day to day.* Often, these tests simply corroborate what teachers already know, but sometimes new information is provided that can have a positive influence on teaching practices. On a larger scale, to comprehensively evaluate programs and schools, standardized tests have value because of their technical soundness and their ability to identify strengths and weaknesses, show gains from year to year, and compare programs to establish effectiveness.

8

_____

Grading

In this chapter, we will consider fundamental principles about grading—that pervasive practice of using marks to communicate something about student performance to students, parents, teachers, and others. As a type of professional judgment, grading is fraught with limitations and conflicting purposes, and there is considerable variability in how different teachers weight factors in determining grades. Indeed, research has documented for years that grading tends to be a "hodgepodge" of various inputs (Brookhart, 2004; Cizek, Rachor, & Fitzgerald, 1996). There is simply a lot of variability in grading practices. For such an important practice (grades are high stakes!), there is little consistency across schools and classrooms, even when teachers use the same grading scale and have the same grading guidelines. There is also much misunderstanding about various approaches to grading. The latest influence on different approaches, standards-based education, makes it more important than ever to reflect on why we grade, what effect grading has on students, and what approaches to grading have the most benefits. First, a word or two about the key role of teachers' judgments in the grading process.

TEACHERS' JUDGMENTS

Grading is not objective. There are various inputs that teachers use that are scored objectively (e.g., multiple-choice tests), but these are used with other subjective judgments to arrive at grades for individual tests, papers, and projects, and for grades at the end of a semester. These judgments include

- The determination of the difficulty of test items
- What is covered on a test

- Whether extra credit will be included
- How scores of different assessments are weighted and combined
- How effort and improvement are included
- The determination of percentages of students obtaining different grades
- The determination of criteria for evaluating papers, performance assessments, and portfolios

In addition to these factors there are unforeseen, unique situations constantly arise, and these situations require teacher judgment. Consider the following case:

Final course grades for Ms. Lorenno's fifth grade classroom include quizzes, tests, participation in class, and homework. One of her best students, Ashley, obtained an A on all the quizzes and tests, obtained satisfactory scores for participation, but failed to hand in homework. Ashley's calculated overall score at the end of the semester was 92.7, which, according to the district grading scale, was a B+.

Is the B+ the correct grade? Should Ashley get an A since that's what she scored on the tests, the best assessment of what she knew? Is it fair to average in zeros for homework? Isn't "participation" too subjective to include? The answers to these questions depend on many factors, not the least of which is the teacher's value system. Often the value system of teachers conflicts with what is mandated by high-stakes accountability testing. Teacher values and beliefs provide a rationale for using practices that are consistent with what is most important in the teaching/learning process. High-stakes accountability tests are only concerned with a summative score that represents proficiency. Teachers are concerned with learning and motivation during the school year, and use grades to reflect all that students are engaged with. As a consequence, grades are often inconsistent with results from large-scale accountability tests. The bottom line is that teachers' values, subjective evaluations, decisions, beliefs, philosophy of education, and intuition are used in grading. These influences cannot be excluded because they are essential to the nature of evaluation of student knowledge and skills day in and day out in the classroom.

PURPOSES OF GRADING

One of the most important inputs that determine grading practices is being clear about the purpose for assigning grades to student work. We will consider five major purposes: communicating student learning, ranking students, providing feedback to students, motivating students, and evaluating teaching and curriculum. With these myriad purposes it is no wonder grading practices are so varied.

Communicating Student Learning

The primary reason for grading is to provide students, parents, and other educators with information about the achievement of learning objectives, goals, and standards. This is usually accomplished by using letter grades on tests, papers, and other student products. This is essentially summative evaluation— documentation of what students have learned in relation to established standards or other students, culminating in report cards and reporting systems. An important issue with this purpose is how much of the grade is based solely on demonstrated student learning, and how much effort, improvement, participation, and other non-achievement factors are included. Often grades for individual student products, whether these are quizzes, tests, or papers, are based mostly if not solely on student performance. When these individual marks are combined for a semester grade or for some other reporting system, however, more subjective factors are often considered, such as extra-credit, retesting, revising, participation, and improvement.

Grading that is determined by the student's level of performance is called *standards-based, criterion-referenced, mastery,* or *absolute* grading. This kind of grading is based on comparing student performance to established levels of knowledge, understanding, and skills. The focus is on communicating performance as it relates to the learning targets and standards. It doesn't matter how a student compares to other students or how much the student has improved, only how he or she compares with the levels of performance. This kind of grading is at the heart of standards-based education.

Ranking Students

A longstanding grading issue is whether a grade is based on a comparison to the performance of other students or to established targets and standards. Historically, grades have reflected both kinds of comparisons. A norm-referenced element in grading has been important because it ranks students (e.g., "grading on the curve"). This allows determination of the "best" and "worse" student. This kind of information is needed for selection to subsequent settings for students, whether it is an honors class in high school, college admissions, or employment. Most current grading scales still emphasize ranking by describing a C grade as "average" and a B as "above average". "Average" can only be determined by comparison to others. The reality is that some degree of sorting must be included in grading and must be reflected to some extent in final grades. The "highest" or "best" students need to be identified. Not all children can get an A.

Numerically, the average depends on the distribution of scores. The question is whether that distribution is based on an individual class or some other group. This means that the "standard" set by the distribution could change from class to class. So, in an honors class the students in the middle of the scores would get a C? Does that make sense? Not really, just like it doesn't make sense that students achieving the highest score in a remedial class get As. These are situations where teachers adjust comparisons based on student ability, by how difficult the tests are, and by how tough they grade papers, projects, and other products. Yet another circumstance that requires teacher judgment!

The reality of needing to rank students is theoretically inconsistent with the idea of high standards and No Child Left Behind (NCLB). With standards-based education, theoretically, all students can perform to meet the standard. In this sense they *could* all receive the same grade. The approach of standards-based education that deals with this inconsistency is to set a goal of "proficient" and then have advanced categories that signify that students have gone beyond the proficient standard in what they know, understand, and can do. Consequently, a proficient rating may translate to a B, and an advanced rating an A.

Providing Feedback

When teachers give grades they have the opportunity to provide feedback to students about how well, and in what ways, proficiency was demonstrated. This kind of information is important for helping students understand why they received a specific grade, and, when specified in sufficient detail, providing information about where there were mistakes, areas of strength and weakness, and what further steps would increase proficiency. It is used to reduce the discrepancy between current and desired proficiency. Doling out praise, rewards, or punishments is not feedback, nor are comparisons with other students (Hattie & Timperley, 2007).

Feedback is usually delivered in three ways. One approach is to have a specific narrative that accompanies each possible grade. This is what we try to do with standards-based education. A second technique is to provide oral or written comments along with a grade. If these comments are individualized and specific they can be very important for motivating students and identifying what further learning is needed. General feedback, such as "good job" or "keep up the good work," is not very helpful because it is not unique or specific. With targeted comments, students focus on what learning needs to be accomplished, rather than trying to interpret the meaning of a letter grade.

When grades and feedback are provided on an ongoing basis, as part of formative assessment, the nature of the feedback is especially important (Black, Harrison, Lee, Marshall, & Wiliam, 2003). Feedback that is specific, targeted, and immediate provides the information students need to improve. It is how students know if their work matches up with the standard and what else is needed to meet the standard. It helps students understand the nature of the target or standard as well as the criteria that are used for evaluation. Used in this way, grades are more than a judgment about what has occurred in the past. They also mean something about what further action is needed. Also, students are encouraged to be self-monitoring and self-reflecting to become adept at error detection.

Motivating Students

One way or another, grades motivate students. But the nature of the motivation can be quite different, depending on whether it is intrinsically or extrinsically oriented. If grades are viewed as extrinsic rewards for successful performance, students are motivated by the rewards received, not by improving themselves. With such *performance goals,* students exert effort to get a high grade, pass, or score higher than other students. This kind of reward, like achieving a "proficient" rating on a high-stakes test, encourages summative judgments, which focus on extrinsic rewards and compliance in the management of student behavior.

With a *mastery* or *learning goal* orientation, students are motivated by a desire to improve their knowledge, understanding, and skills; getting the reward is secondary. As a result, learning and motivation is more intrinsic. Students see the value in what is being learned. Students with a mastery orientation learn more, prefer more challenging tasks, stay engaged longer, display independent learning, have more positive attitudes toward learning, become more motivated toward success rather than failure-avoiding, and see the connection between their effort and successful learning. The advantages of having a more mastery goal orientation are substantial. And yet, testing practices promote more of a performance orientation.

Another important component of motivation is *self-efficacy.* Self-efficacy refers to the extent to which students believe they are capable of successful performance. It is close to a sense of ability. A strong sense of self-efficacy leads to greater motivation because students think they can achieve and do well. It makes it more likely that they will initiate actions that will lead to success. Self-efficacy is strengthened when grades communicate to students that their success is internal, due to either their own effort or ability, or some combination of effort and ability. Such explanations of success establish a belief that they are able to do well. Self-efficacy is also strengthened when comments accompanying grades specifically address the contribution of their ability when investing moderate and high levels of effort.

Evaluating Teaching and Curriculum

A fifth purpose for grading is to provide information that informs the teacher about the success of the instruction and the curriculum. When teachers use grades as feedback to themselves, the information shows strengths and weaknesses in instruction. This is dependent on having grades at a focused, relatively narrow level. For example, giving grades for weekly tests is more likely to give the teacher good feedback than a six weeks test because the weekly tests are generally more specific to what was taught. When evaluated more frequently, teachers can compare grade distributions in light of teaching activities to help diagnose needed changes in instruction. More broadly, curriculum can be evaluated with grades representing learning outcomes. If lower grades are associated with a particular curriculum, the grades are evidence that the curriculum is not maximizing student learning. Granted, there are many influences on student learning, but grades can give an indication of effectiveness of the teaching and/or curriculum.

INCLUSION OF ACADEMIC ENABLERS

One of the most difficult issues in grading is what to do with factors such as effort, work habits, willingness to participate, group skills, motivation, and cooperative group peer teaching skills. I call these factors *academic enablers* because they are important to being able to demonstrate proficiency, and are traits that teachers cultivate because they are important for influencing student engagement, attitudes, and ultimately achievement. Some teachers believe that hard work and participation *are* learning, and are showing student proficiency. While this may be true, especially when teachers are able to see that effort results in higher achievement, direct measures of academic enablers are difficult, to say the least, especially in a systematic way with strong reliability.

Effort is perhaps the most important academic enabler, and many if not most teachers use some measure of effort in their grading. After all, aren't students who try hard learning more than students who don't try hard? Then there are life skills that teachers think are important to instill, such as self-discipline, dependability, punctuality, and work completion. These characteristics and others need to be an integral part of what students learn. The issue is how this affects grading. Some teachers integrate such skills into academic grades. It makes more sense, though, to give separate grades for these types of assessment.

STANDARDS-BASED GRADING

There are a number of approaches to grading, including the use of letters, pass/fail, and checklists—each with advantages and disadvantages. What we will focus on here is standards-based grading, since this is what is now occurring in most classrooms. Standards-based grading has four essential characteristics (Guskey & Bailey, 2001): (1) pre-established, well-defined standards; (2) identification of the best evidence that shows progress toward meeting the standards; (3) pre-established, high levels of performance for all students and benchmarks; and (4) clearly articulated conversions from levels of performance to grades and reports that indicate progress toward meeting the standards.

As a direct descendent of criterion-referenced grading, standards-based grading emphasizes the evaluation of student performance in relation to levels of performance on the standard. Thus, how the levels of performance are determined and defined is critical to using this approach. If standards and levels of performance are too general, feedback associated with performance may not be sufficiently detailed to allow for effective feedback. If too specific and numerous, reporting is cumbersome, time consuming, and difficult for parents to understand. Something in the middle is needed.

Performance indicators are used as descriptors that indicate the status of student performance in relation to standard. The descriptors are rank ordered from poor performance to very strong performance. Here are some examples:

Beginning, progressing, proficient, and exceptional

Novice, intermediate, advanced, superior

Needs improvement, proficient, advanced

Absent, developing, adequate, fully developed

Emerging, developing, achieving

Limited, some, nearly complete, complete

Unsatisfactory, satisfactory, very good, excellent, outstanding

Some performance indicators use a scale that indicates how frequently different proficiencies were displayed, using terms such as *seldom, sometimes, frequently,* or *consistently*.

Typically, each descriptor is aligned with a letter grade, as illustrated in Table 8.1. The matches between scale descriptors and letter grades are arbitrary. What one person may think constitutes a B another person might think describes a C. There is almost complete focus on academic performance. This does not leave much room for academic enablers (e.g., effort, progress), though in my experience teachers find a way to include them.

Note that there is no provision for student-to-student comparison, nor is there any provision for improvement over time. What is stressed is proficiency on the standard. It doesn't matter how much students *learned* or *changed* to be able to demonstrate that proficiency. This is counterintuitive to the way many think about education, as taking students from point A to point B. It means that

Table 8.1 Examples of Standards-Based Grades

Grade	Descriptions
A	Outstanding, advanced, exceptional: complete knowledge of all content; mastery of all standards
B	Very good: better than proficient; complete knowledge of most content; mastery of most standards
C	Proficient or acceptable: some knowledge; some mastery of standards
D	Making progress or developing: lacks knowledge of most content; mastery of only a few standards
F	Unsatisfactory: lacks knowledge of content; no mastery of standards

some students who make great progress during a year, but still don't perform at a proficient level, are not recognized for their hard work and achievement. And, teachers of these students may be sanctioned when in fact they were instrumental in moving the student to a higher level of proficiency.

A concept called *value-added* education is currently being considered to account for a change in proficiency. This approach is used for accountability in some locations and may become a feature of standards-based education. The "standard" may become some level of improvement or change. This would be a welcome change in standards-based education that would more realistically reflect and encourage effective teaching.

Percentage-Based Grading

The most common approach for standards-based grading is called *percentage-based*. This is because test and quiz scores can readily be translated to percentage-correct indices, and most school districts use a percentage-based grading scale. The number refers to the percentage of items answered correctly or points out of a possible 100. Different percentages of correct answers or performance are used to assign grades, for example,

A: 94–100

B: 86–93

C: 75–85

D: 65–74

F: Below 65

So, if a student gets 80 percent of the items correct, the grade is a C. The determination of using 75 to 85 percent as the C category is also arbitrary. In another school district, the C range could be 70 to 80 percent. What, then, is done with papers, performance assessments, and portfolios that don't have "items" that can be used to calculate the percentage correct? Typically, each grade is aligned with a score (e.g., A = 100; A– = 95; B+ = 90, etc.), which is then combined with test scores.

Percentage-based grading is both easy and familiar. What needs to be considered, though, is the effect of item difficulty. The difficulty of the item has a direct relationship to what percentage correct means. Simply put, a score of 80 on a hard test means something different than a score of 80 on an easy test. It is quite possible, even probable, that two teachers, given the same learning target or standard, will construct tests that are unequal with respect to item difficulty. This is most likely to occur with teacher-constructed multiple-choice tests, the kind of test that mimics large-scale accountability tests.

Consider the following example. Mr. Trent is teaching American geography, and one of his learning targets is concerned with knowing characteristics of different regions. He is using a multiple-choice test and comes up with this item:

Which of the following is a *plains* state?

a. Chicago

b. Miami

c. North Dakota

d. Maine

This is obviously an easy item. Here is one that tests the same target but is more difficult.

Which of the following is a *plains* state?

a. Michigan

b. California

c. North Dakota

d. Mississippi

The point is that the percentage-correct grading scale makes sense only when you understand the difficulty of the items. This has a direct bearing on the grades given. One of the challenges of assessment is to estimate item difficulty before students take the test. This typically depends on how other students have scored on similar items in the past. For example, if one of your high aptitude classes works hard to learn the content but then gets a low score on the test, then the items in that test are probably difficult. A low-aptitude class that obtains a high score probably means that the items are easy. What happens when a teacher uses a test or substantial number of new items on a semester exam, and the class scores low, lower than other assessments given during the semester? In this circumstance it may be most fair to make adjustments so that the distribution of scores reflects the range of student achievement demonstrated throughout the semester. Otherwise, the single exam score will have an unfair effect of lowering grades. It would not be fair, however, to make the adjustment by designating the top score 100, and then recalculating the remaining scores. This relies too heavily on the performance of a single student.

The irony of the practice of using a percentage-correct approach is that what is perceived to be "high" or "tough" may actually be just the opposite. A grading scale that seems "hard" requires an 86 or better to obtain a B (harder than a scale where an 80 will result in a B). One way to ensure that a high percentage of students obtain a B or better is to use easy test items. For a more "generous" scale, test items would typically be more difficult. As pointed out earlier, more challenging items affect student study habits and motivation.

Determining Composite Grades

Combining individual scores obtained from tests, quizzes, homework, papers, etc. so that there is a single, overall score is what teachers do for six-weeks, nine-weeks, or semester grades. Three steps are taken to arrive at these composite scores and corresponding grades: (1) select what will be included in the final grade; (2) select weights for each individual assessment; and (3) combine the weighted scores to determine the single, overall grade.

Select What to Include

Teachers typically have a fair amount of leeway in deciding what assessments to include in the final grade. In standards-based education there is heavy reliance on assessments that directly measure important targets, such as tests, but decisions still have to be made about homework, quizzes, participation, papers, projects, presentations, and other evidence of student learning. The decision about what to include should be based primarily on two considerations. The first is the extent to which the assessment of student performance is directly related to the standards. It makes sense that a unit test of knowledge that aligns with the standard would be included. What about pop quizzes and homework? Do these assessments legitimately serve as documentation of student learning and understanding? If they are primarily formative in nature, to provide students with practice and opportunities for feedback, they may be considered as instruction more than an assessment. Some teachers feel that pop quizzes are not fair, and obviously we don't know for sure who completes homework assignments. Since participation in class is influenced by group dynamics and student personalities, would it be considered formative rather than summative? Some teachers maintain that participation, engagement, and other indicators of effort are evidence of learning, and would include scores on these behaviors in calculating final grades.

The final decision about what to include should be made on what the grade means. If the grade is intended to indicate *only* student proficiency in relation to a learning standard, then academic enablers should not be included. Suppose a student does not complete homework but otherwise does very well on tests. Should a zero be included, something that is more a measure of responsibility than achievement? Not if the final grade is an indicator of only proficiency on the standard. The reality, of course, is that homework usually *is* included as a formative assessment that is primarily used as a way to motivate students and provide the teacher with information that can be used to direct further instruction. What about work habits, determination, cooperativeness, and other academic enablers? These factors are important to the learning process and allow teachers to reinforce internal attributions and student responsibility for achievement, so my view is that they can legitimately be included in calculating composite scores. Others argue that using academic enablers is fraught with difficulty, including being hard to assess, prone to giving students a false sense of achievement, being open to teacher bias, and subject to student faking. Clearly, academic enablers shouldn't be able to mask or affect greatly scores from major assessments of student performance.

If academic enablers are used, it is important to include all factors that are used to determine the grades in a description of what the grades mean. It is also a good practice to create scoring rubrics for effort and other academic enablers and also provide students with feedback based on the rubrics.

Some schools, especially elementary schools, provide for separate assessment, grading, and reporting of academic enablers. This is a great approach but it is not without limitations. Besides being time consuming to gather and report the information, grading these factors separately suggests that they do not indicate academic performance, when in fact they may. It also requires separate evidence and justifications, with a higher standard of reliability and validity than when the factors are included in one grade.

A final consideration when determining what to include is the need to consider how many different assessments are needed. While most would agree that a single assessment (e.g., final exam) is not sufficient for an extended unit of study, there is no agreement about what would be best. The general rule of thumb is that grades will be more accurate when they are based on many different assessments and different types of assessments. As pointed out by Marzano (2006), systematic use of assessments can have a positive impact on student learning. This doesn't mean, though, that an assessment every day is best! For a semester grade, obviously more assessments are needed, while for a six weeks grade, fewer. One rule of thumb is to think about one major test and at least two other assessments every two weeks. Once again, professional judgment is needed, based on subject, grade level, and students. One teacher might have three major assessments for a six weeks grade while another down the hall has ten assessments.

Determine Weights

Once the assessments to be included have been identified, there is a need to determine how much weight each one should contribute to the composite score. More important assessments get greater weight, indicated by the percentage they contribute to the final grade. So, it may be that chapter and unit tests contribute 80 percent, with homework and quizzes 10 percent each. Greatest weight should be given to assessments that give the strongest evidence of student proficiency—those that align closely with the standards and reflect instructional time during the learning process.

It is best to align different segments of content over the instructional period to be roughly consistent with the emphasis of different areas tested. This is a type of content-related evidence for validity. With a nine weeks grade of student proficiency in knowledge of American history since 1900, weight on separate assessments during the nine weeks should be consistent with what is intended to be covered as well as what was covered. Suppose 50 percent of the standard, when breaking out this historical period, concerns political events. Chapter tests and quizzes of political events should be weighted so that they contribute 50 percent to the final grade. That is, the overall goal is to weigh assessments to match percentages attributed to topics in the standards tested so that the grade reflects the relative contribution of each topic.

While instructional time is not a factor in determining weights according to alignment, as discussed above, it is an important barometer of the amount of emphasis given to each topic, and as such should be considered. For example, if 50 percent of instructional time during a nine week period in a biology class is spent on invertebrates, it probably isn't reasonable if only 15 percent of the grade is based on that topic. Often, the amount of time devoted to a topic, and hence it's weight, is known only during or after the instructional period. This means that weights are best determined at the end of this period, rather than at the beginning of the unit.

Combine Scores

After weights have been determined, the percentage of correct figures are combined mathematically to come up with an overall percentage that is then converted to a grade. Since the scale is the same for all assessments, it is simply a matter of multiplying each percentage score by the appropriate weight. So, if an exam score is 50 percent of the final grade, the percentage for that test is multiplied by .50 (e.g., if the percent correct is 80 percent, multiplying by .50 gives a score of 40). This score is added to the others that are collected to result in an overall composite score, which then corresponds to a letter grade. Consider the following nine week's scores from Jamie and Shimeka on several assessments, with designated weights. The tests percentage correct was converted from raw scores to a percentage out of 100. So, if the unit test had 50 items, the raw score is multiplied by two.

Assessment	Weight	Jamie % Correct	Shimeka % Correct
Unit test	40%	70	60
Chapter test	30%	80	75
Paper	30%	90	80
Homework	10%	70	100
Composite Score		**86**	**80.5**

To arrive at the composite score, multiply each percent correct by the corresponding weight, as a decimal, and add all the products. Jamie would receive a composite score of 86:

$$(70 \times .4) + (80 \times .3) + (90 \times .3) + (70 \times .1) = 28 + 24 + 27 + 7 = 86$$

Shimeka's composite score would be

$$(60 \times .4) + (75 \times .3) + (80 \times .3) + (100 \times .1) = 24 + 22.5 + 24 + 10 = 80.5$$

If the grading scale is 87–94 = B and 80–87 = C, then both students would receive the same letter grade (assuming no pluses or minuses). Both students used assessments other than tests to rescue low test scores. For Jamie, it was the paper; for Shimeka, the paper and homework. But is it valid to conclude that Jamie and Shimeka are about the same in relation to proficiency on the standard or target represented by grade received? No matter how much scores are converted, weighted, multiplied, and added, there is often this rather "soft" but important judgment. With grading software it is really easy to have these calculations completed, with a contention that the grading was "objective." But nothing is more unfair than mindless number crunching. There are simply too many influences on grades that cannot be accounted for with grading software. How are borderline scores handled? What about improvement? Should a good final comprehensive exam cancel out poor chapter tests? What if the weights were different?

The most egregious, widespread error with number crunching grades is giving a zero for work not completed. Suppose Jamie did not hand in a paper and was given a zero. Her composite score would go from 86 to 59, from a high C to F. The question is, is this F a fair indication of her proficiency on the target or standard? Definitely not! If a student is able to do as well as she did on the chapter and unit test, an F is not a valid indicator. Because the range of a zero to a score meriting a D is so large (e.g., 70 points), and the range between other letter grades is about 7 points, a zero has the effect of multiplying by 10 the impact of the zero on the composite score. What happens is that a nonachievement factor—responsibility—is now a major contributor to the grade. One approach for avoiding this pitfall is to tell students that they will get a "zero" if they do not turn in work, but use 60 or 65 as the score that is included in calculating the composite. This still motivates students, which is what the threat of a zero does, but does not have such a catastrophic impact on the composite score.

One aspect of grading that is not captured with percentage-correct calculations is how to handle improvement over time. In standards-based education this can be a significant issue. Suppose a teacher has a final, comprehensive exam that includes knowledge and skills from the entire instructional period.

There may be smaller quizzes along the way, but the final is clearly the best and final measure of all learning targets. If a student scores very low on the quizzes but very high on the final, why wouldn't it make sense to award the student an A, regardless of the scores on the quiz? Obviously the performance of the student shows that he or she is highly proficient on the standard being measured. In this kind of case, improvement should be considered.

Assign Total Points

Another popular method of calculating grades is called *total points*. This approach, which is mathematically equivalent to the percentage-based method, is done by giving each assessment points and adding the points obtained for all assessments to obtain a number that is compared to the total possible points. The number of points assigned to each assessment is done to reflect the weight of each assessment. For example, a unit grade may be based on an overall total of 250 points. The exam has 100 possible points, the book report 50 points, homework 50 points (10 points for each week), and a research paper has 50 points. If the grading scale is 95–100 for an A, students must obtain at least 238 points (95 percent of 250). In this example, the exam is weighted at 40 percent of the final grade; the other 60 percent is equally divided among the book report, homework, and research paper. Of course, in some cases, students may be 1 point shy of a higher grade. That brings up another important issue in grading—borderline scores.

Grade Borderline Scores

There are many cases of grading scores that are "borderline," or right on the dividing line between two letter grades. Suppose a student obtains a composite score of 89.4 but needs 89.6 to be rounded to 90 to get an A. Or maybe a student is 2 points out of 300 away from a higher grade. Borderline scores that just make it to the higher level are not an issue. Research has shown that teachers want their students to get the highest possible grade and look for things like improvement, participation, extra credit, and retakes of tests to get students over the hump. One approach to grading that lessens the number of borderline grades is to use pluses and minuses. This allows for greater discrimination among students. Rather than deciding between an A and a B, using A– and B+ provides more options that can more realistically portray student proficiency. My approach to borderline grades is to give students the benefit of the doubt when very close to a higher grade. There is error in every type of assessment we use, and it is possible that some of that error resulted in a score that is lower than the students' actual level of proficiency.

Effective Grading

I have had two major objectives in this chapter. First, I wanted to stress the importance of teachers' professional judgments when constructing and implementing a grading system. There is no completely objective way to grade students and come up with final semester or course grades. Grading is professional decision making that depends on the values, philosophies, and perspectives of teachers and external pressures such as high-stakes accountability testing. Second, grading needs to be considered within the larger context of principles of learning and motivation, effective teaching, and development of important life skills and attitudes that go beyond what is required to demonstrate proficiency on accountability tests. In this spirit, Table 8.2 lists some "do's and don'ts" of effective grading.

Table 8.2   Do's and Don'ts of Effective Grading

Do	Don't
Grade according to pre-established learning targets and standards	Grade on the curve
Grade fairly	Allow personal bias to affect grades
Use reasonable and justified professional judgment	Rely entirely on number crunching
Base grades primarily on student performance on assessments of targets and standards	Use effort, attitudes, engagement, participation, and other academic enablers as major sources for determining grades
Review borderline scores carefully; when in doubt, give the higher grade	Be inflexible about borderline cases
Use a sufficient number of assessments (at least one a week)	Use a small number of assessments
Rely most on recent student performance	Penalize students who perform poorly early in the marking period by making it difficult for them to obtain a high grade.
Have a clear, well-articulated grading policy	Grade haphazardly
Be willing to change grades when warranted	Be inflexible and resistant to changing grades
Minimize the impact of zeros	Use zeros indiscriminately when calculating composite scores

References

Airasian, P. W. (1997). *Classroom assessment* (3rd ed.). New York: McGraw-Hill.

Ames, C. (1992). Classrooms: Goals, structures, and student motivation. *Journal of Educational Psychology, 84,* 261–271.

Anderson, L. W., & Krathwohl, D. R. (2001). *A taxonomy for learning, teaching, and assessing: A revisions of Bloom's taxonomy of educational objectives.* Boston: Allyn & Bacon.

Black, P., Harrison, C., Lee, C., Marshall, B., & Wiliam, D. (2003). *Assessment for learning: Putting it into practice.* Berkshire, England: Open University Press.

Black, P., & Wiliam, D. (1998). Assessment and classroom learning. *Assessment in Education, 5*(1), 103–110.

Bloom, B. S. (1956). *Taxonomy of educational objectives: The classification of educational goals, Handbook 1, cognitive domain.* New York: David McKay.

Brookhart, S. M. (2004). *Grading.* Upper Saddle River, NJ: Prentice Hall.

Cizek, G. J. (1997). Learning, achievement, and assessment: Constructs at a crossroads. In G. D. Phyc (Ed.), *Handbook of classroom assessment: Learning, adjustment, and achievement* (pp. 1–32). San Diego: Academic Press.

Cizek, G. J., Rachor, R. E., & Fitzgerald, S. M. (1996). Teachers' assessment practices: Preparation, isolation, and the kitchen sink. *Educational Assessment, 3*(2), 159–179.

CTB/McGraw-Hill. (1997). *TerraNova: Individual profile report and class record sheet.* New York: McGraw-Hill.

Dweck, C. S., & Leggett, E. L. (1988). A social-cognitive approach to motivation and personality. *Psychological Review, 95,* 256–273.

Gardner, H. (1993). *Multiple intelligences: Theory into practice.* New York: Basic Books.

Guskey, T. R., & Bailey, J. M. (2001). *Developing grading and reporting systems for student learning.* Thousand Oaks, CA: Corwin Press.

Hattie, J., & Timperley, H. (2007). The power of feedback. *Review of Educational Research, 77*(1), 81–112.

Heubert, J. P., & Hauser, R. M. (Eds.). (1999). *High stakes testing for tracking, promotion, and graduation.* Washington, DC: National Academy Press.

Impara, J. C., & Plake, B. S. (1996). Professional development in student assessment for educational administrators. *Educational Measurement: Issues and Practice, 15*(2), 14–19.

Marzano, R. J. (2006). *Classroom assessment and grading that work.* Alexandria, VA: Association of Supervision and Curriculum Development.

Marzano, R. J., & Kendall, J. S. (1996). *A comprehensive guide to designing standards-based districts, schools, and classrooms.* Alexandria, VA: Association for Supervision & Curriculum Development.

Marzano, R. J., & Kendall, J. S. (2007). *The new taxonomy of educational objectives* (2nd ed.). Thousand Oaks, CA: Corwin Press.

McMillan, J. H. (1999). *Teachers' classroom assessment and grading practices: Phase 2.* Richmond, VA: Metropolitan Educational Research Consortium, Virginia Commonwealth University.

McMillan, J. H. (2007a). *Classroom assessment: Principles and practice for effective instruction* (4th ed.). Boston: Allyn & Bacon.

McMillan, J. H. (2007b). Formative classroom assessment: The key to improving student achievement. In J. H. McMillan (Ed.), *Formative classroom assessment* (pp. 1–7). New York: Teachers College Press.

McMillan, J. H., & Schumacher, S. (2006). *Research in education: A conceptual introduction* (6th ed.). Boston: Pearson Education Inc.

Messick, S. (1989). Validity. In R. L. Linn (Ed.), *Educational measurement* (3rd ed.) (pp. 13–103). New York: American Council of Education/Macmillan.

Messick, S. (1995). Validity of psychological assessment: Validation of inferences from persons' responses and performances as scientific inquiry into score meaning. *American Psychologist, 50,* 741–749.

Moss, P. A., Girard, B. J., & Haniford, L. C. (2006). Validity in educational assessment. In J. Green & A. Luke (Eds.), *Review of research in education 30.* Washington, DC: American Educational Research Association.

Pearson Education. (2007). *Improving Student Achievement Meeting Key Performance Measures.* Retrieved May 12, 2007, from http://formative.pearsonassessments.com/about/index.htm

Pintrich, P. R., & Schunk, D. H. (1996). *Motivation in education: Theory, research, and applications.* Englewood Cliffs, NJ: Prentice Hall.

Popham, W. J. (1997). Consequential validity: Right concern—wrong concept. *Educational Measurement: Issues and Practice, 16*(2), 9–13.

Popham, W. J. (2006). All about accountability/phony formative assessments: Buyer beware! *Educational Leadership, 64*(3), 86–87.

Popham, W. J. (2007). *Classroom assessment: What teachers need to know* (5th ed.). Boston: Allyn & Bacon.

Shepard, L. A. (1997). The centrality of test use and consequences for test validity. *Educational Measurement: Issues and Practice, 16*(2), 5–8, 13, 24.

Standards for teacher competence in educational assessment of students. (1990). Washington, DC: National Council on Measurement in Education.

Sternberg, R. J. (1985). *Beyond IQ: A triarchic theory of intelligence.* Cambridge, UK: Cambridge University Press.

Tombari, M. L., & Borich, G. D. (1999). *Authentic assessment in the classroom: Applications and practice.* Upper Saddle River, NJ: Prentice Hall.

Virginia Department of Education Web site. Retrieved March 30, 2007, from http://www.doe.virginia.gov/VDOE/assessment/home.shtonl#sol_administration_manuals

Whittington, D. (1999). Making room for values and fairness: Teaching reliability and validity in the classroom context. *Educational Measurement: Issues and Practice, 18*(1), 14–22, 27.

Wiggins, G., & McTighe, J. (2005). *Understanding by design* (2nd ed.). Alexandria, VA: Association of Supervision and Curriculum Development.

Wiliam, D., & Leahy, S. (2007). A theoretical foundation for formative assessment. In J. H. McMillan (Ed.), *Formative classroom assessment.* New York: Teachers College Press.

Wood, J. (1992). *Adapting instruction for mainstreamed and at-risk students.* Upper Saddle River, NJ: Prentice-Hall.

Index

performance assessment,
88–90
portfolios, 91
ranked scores, 96, 97
raw scores, 11, 96, 97,
129–130, 134
relative derived scores, 130
school-wide scores, 6
spread of, 47, 47–48 (figures), 50
stability of, 39–40
standards-based test scores,
134–137, 135 (table)
standard scores, 11, 131,
132 (table)
stereotyping and, 65
subjectivity in scoring, 82, 83
tied scores, 97
See also Assessment methods;
Grading; Numerical data;
Reliability; Validity
Selected-response assessment,
12–13, 13 (table), 14, 49,
75–76, 76 (tables)
binary-choice items, 80–81,
81 (table)
difficulty index and, 113
matching items, 79–80,
80 (table)
multiple-choice items, 77–79,
78 (table)
See also Assessment methods;
Constructed-response
assessment
Self-assessment. *See* Student
self-assessment
Self-efficacy, 147
Self-report instrument, 24
Sentence completion tests,
13 (table)
Short answer items, 13 (table), 68,
75, 76 (tables)
Showcase portfolios, 91
Simple frequency distribution, 97
Skill assessment, 13
Socioeconomic status. *See* Bias;
Fairness
Spearman, C., 125
Special needs students, 6, 66–69,
67 (table), 139, 141
Spurious correlation, 109
Stability estimates of reliability,
39–40
Standard Age Score, 132 (table)
Standard deviation, 103, 131
calculation of, 104–106,
104–106 (figures)
normal curves and, 104, 104
(figure)
See also Measures of
dispersion; Numerical
data

Standard error of measurement
(SEM), 50
Standard scores, 11, 131, 132
(table)
Standardized tests, 2–3
ability tests, 4, 10 (figure), 119,
124–126, 127 (table)
achievement tests, 10 (figure),
24–26, 25 (table), 39, 41,
119, 121–123
banks of items and, 10,
10 (figure), 123
benchmark tests, 10
derived scores and, 97
externally mandated tests,
1, 3, 4
formative assessment and,
10–11, 10 (figure)
high-stakes testing, 3, 28, 32,
40, 46, 120, 128, 144
item response theory and, 40
pilot testing of, 11
quantitative measurement
and, 11
school-wide scores, 6
score interpretation and, 1,
126, 128, 129–137, 132
(table),
135 (table)
state tests, 10 (figure)
teacher effectiveness and, 20,
139, 141
validity issues and, 24–26,
25 (table)
See also Assessment;
Assessment methods;
Large-scale tests;
Measurement;
National/state large-scale
tests; Reliability;
Standards-based
education; Validity
Standards of Learning (SOL),
25, 25 (table)
Standards-based education, 3–4
adequate progress
requirements and, 3
assessment, purpose/nature
of, 6, 13
assessment standards, 16–18
content standards, 3, 25–26
evaluation/interpretation of
assessment results, 13–14
formative assessment and, 7, 8
(table), 9–10, 9–10
(figures)
large-scale tests and, 4, 5,
6–7, 8 (table)
legislation for, 3
local assessments and, 4, 4
(figure), 5, 6–7, 8 (table)

measurement/assessment
methods and, 11–13,
13 (table)
performance standards, 3
summative assessment and, 7,
8 (table), 10–11,
10 (figure)
teaching practices, assessment
and, 5, 5 (figure), 7
testing requirements and, 3
See also Assessment;
Assessment methods;
Grading; Instruction;
National/state large-scale
tests; Reliability;
Standardized tests;
Student learning; Validity
Standards-based grading, 145,
148–150, 149 (table)
composite grades,
computation of, 152–156
percentage-based grading,
150–152
See also Grading
Standards-based interpretations,
45–46, 134–137, 135 (table)
Standards-referenced
assessments, 14, 113,
123–124
score interpretation, 129–137,
132 (table), 135 (table)
See also National/state
large-scale tests
Stanford Achievement Test
Series, 121
Stanford-Binet Scale, 125, 126,
127 (table)
Stanine, 132 (table)
STARS. *See* School-based Teacher-
led Assessment and
Reporting System (STARS)
State standards-based tests, 10
(figure), 97
See also National/state large-
scale tests
Statistics. *See* Numerical data
Stereotyping, 63
formative assessment
and, 64–65
prior to instruction/
assessment, 63–64
summative assessment and, 65
See also Bias; Fairness
Sternberg, R. J., 125
Structured interviews, 13 (table)
Structured observation, 13 (table)
Student learning, 1
assessment and, 1, 2, 7,
12, 14, 22
cognitive/constructivist
theories of, 4

CORWIN PRESS

The Corwin Press logo—a raven striding across an open book—represents the union of courage and learning. Corwin Press is committed to improving education for all learners by publishing books and other professional development resources for those serving the field of PreK–12 education. By providing practical, hands-on materials, Corwin Press continues to carry out the promise of its motto: **"Helping Educators Do Their Work Better."**